BAL'S
QUICK & HEALTHY
INDIAN

BAL'S
QUICK & HEALTHY
INDIAN

BAL ARNESON

whitecap

Whitecap Books is known for its expertise in the cookbook
market, and has produced some of the most innovative
and familiar titles found in kitchens across North America.
Visit our website at www.whitecap.ca.

EDITED BY Elaine Jones and Taryn Boyd
COPYEDITED BY Grace Yaginuma and Paula Ayer
DESIGN BY Mauve Pagé
PHOTOGRAPHY BY Tracey Kusiewicz
FOOD STYLING BY Bal Arneson and Tracey Kusiewicz

The publisher would like to thank Denby, a sponsor
of this project.

Tiles in food photographs courtesy of Creekside Tile
Company Ltd. (www.creeksidetile.com).

PRINTED IN Canada at Friesens

LIBRARY AND ARCHIVES CANADA CATALOGUING
IN PUBLICATION

Arneson, Bal, 1972–
   Bal's quick & healthy Indian / Bal Arneson.

Includes index.
ISBN 978-1-77050-023-5

   1. Cooking, Indic. I. Title. II. Title: Bal's quick and
healthy Indian

TX724.5.I4A73 2010   641.5954   C2010-904636-6

The publisher acknowledges the financial support of the
Government of Canada through the Canada Book Fund
(CBF) and the Province of British Columbia through the
Book Publishing Tax Credit.

11 12 13 14 15   5 4 3 2

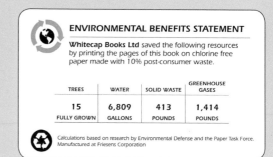

ENVIRONMENTAL BENEFITS STATEMENT

Whitecap Books Ltd saved the following resources
by printing the pages of this book on chlorine free
paper made with 10% post-consumer waste.

TREES	WATER	SOLID WASTE	GREENHOUSE GASES
15	6,809	413	1,414
FULLY GROWN	GALLONS	POUNDS	POUNDS

Calculations based on research by Environmental Defense and the Paper Task Force.
Manufactured at Friesens Corporation

CONTENTS

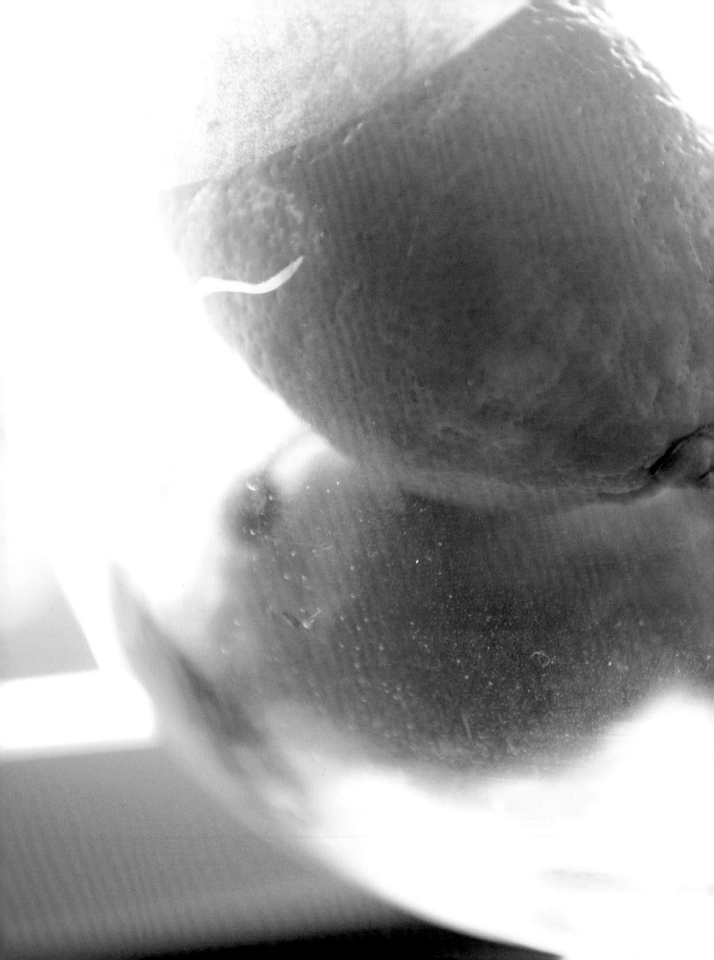

To my lovely children,
Anoop and Aaron,
who inspire me every day,
and to Brad, for his kind,
loving support

PREFACE

EIGHTEEN YEARS AGO I came to Canada from a tiny village in Punjab, India. I learned English and went to school, and eventually achieved my goal of becoming an independent woman with an education and a career—all things I could never have even dreamed of in India. I had left my family behind, but I did bring with me my true love and passion for food. I was very excited to be in North America, and looked forward to exploring food from around the world. I started using traditional Indian spices with main ingredients that were new to me, and my unique cooking style was born—fresh, seasonal, and healthy Indian food.

I was surprised to hear what my North American friends thought about Indian food—creamy, fattening, takes a long time to cook, requires a long list of spices . . . These misconceptions made me think, Wouldn't it be a great idea to write a book that reflects the genuine cooking philosophy of my village—healthy, aromatic, and delicious meals that are quickly and easily prepared? In my village cream and butter were never used on a daily basis; they were considered luxuries and were used only during festivals and special occasions like weddings. In fact, our village recipes were simple and vegetarian. We ate what we had on hand: beans and lentils, fruits, vegetables, and herbs and spices from our own gardens.

The goal of my first cookbook, *Everyday Indian*, was to introduce readers to the kind of Indian food I grew up with. The book reflected the cooking style and methods from the villages of India. When it was first published, I was surprised and very pleased to learn from ayurvedic practitioners that my recipes reflected their ancient principles. Ayurveda emphasizes prevention of disease, rejuvenation of our body systems, and extension of life span. It provides an integrated approach to preventing and treating illness through a holistic lifestyle and natural therapies, such as the use of herbs and spices.

Everyday Indian became a national best-seller within the first eight weeks, and I received an overwhelming, positive response from people around the world. Readers were surprised to learn how healthy Indian food could be, how simple it could be to prepare. People wanted more recipes and asked that my next cookbook provide more health information on the ingredients. I was inspired and set to work on my second cookbook.

It was while I was working on new recipes that I was contacted by a local TV station to do a weekly cooking segment called "Cooking with Bal Arneson." I really enjoyed being in front of the camera, sharing my passion for cooking, and getting such a positive response—within two hours of each segment I would receive more than 11,000 hits on my website and hundreds of emails from viewers! When I shared my enthusiasm with my mentor Chef Michael Smith, he introduced me to his producer, Johanna Eliot. The next

thing I knew I was flying from Vancouver to the other side of Canada—to Halifax—to put together a demo for an Indian cooking show, and then being offered my very own cooking show by the US Cooking Channel and Food Network Canada. We eventually called it *Spice Goddess*. (My 17-year-old daughter, Anoop, came up with the title.)

So many wonderful and amazing blessings have come my way, but what I still appreciate the most is the opportunity to share recipes that take me back to my faraway village. This book is a thank-you gift for all your encouragement and support.

SPICES

"What spices do you have in your pantry?" I have been giving cooking classes for the last 10 years, and this is the question I'm asked the most. I always reply that when I was growing up, my mother basically relied on only two spices: ground turmeric and garam masala (which is a *blend* of spices, but I often think of it as its own spice). And when she wanted to make special dishes for weddings and other festivities, she'd purchase dried fenugreek leaves and cumin seeds from the market. Turmeric, garam masala, fenugreek leaves, and cumin: these particular spices are so flavorful, aromatic, and versatile that there is no limit to their creative combinations, and I often limit myself to just these four, like my mother did. On occasion, I also play with other spices as it's fascinating to cook with them. And, of course, it's important to have a range of spices on hand if you want to make garam masala from scratch!

Here is what I like to keep in my pantry:

Bay leaves are the aromatic leaves of the bay tree. They are usually used in their dried form, and are especially good in tomato-based dishes. Use sparingly as their flavor can be quite strong.

Cardamom pods. The cardamom plant is a tropical bush; the pods are collected and dried, and each pod contains segments of seeds. I use both green and black cardamom; black is a little bit harder to find. It is best to remove the seeds from the outer husks because the husks have no flavor. Once the seeds are ground do not store for too long as the powder rapidly loses its flavor. It is best to grind the seeds as you need to use them. Cardamom is aromatic and has a sweet flavor. (Pictured on page viii.)

Cayenne pepper. A pungent red powder made from dried finely ground pods of various hot red peppers. The level of "heat" usually increases the longer it is cooked.

Cinnamon comes from a tropical evergreen tree. Cinnamon quills are paper-thin layers of bark rolled into cylinders usually referred to as cinnamon sticks. The sticks are a reddish brown color and can be purchased whole or in ground form. Spicy, sweet, and very aromatic.

Cloves are the dried flower buds of a beautiful tropical tree. They have intense flavor but add a pleasant spicy sweetness when used in moderation. Cloves are dark brown in color and can be purchased whole or in ground form.

Coriander is an annual plant; both its leaves and seeds are used to flavor food. The plant produces bright green leaves, which are used as an herb commonly known as cilantro. The seeds of the plant, called coriander seeds, are light tan in color and have a mild pungent flavor. A very useful spice as it goes well with almost any combination of spices.

2

FENNEL SEEDS

FENUGREEK SEEDS

Cumin seeds. Cumin is a small plant that is cultivated in hot climates. The dried seeds are light brown and aromatic. Roasting them lightly before grinding enhances their earthy flavor.

Curry leaves come from a small tropical tree. They are called curry leaves not because of a "curry flavor" but because they are used in curry dishes in South Indian cooking. Curry leaves have a sweet, delicate flavor and can be used fresh or dried. Their full flavor and aroma are extracted by frying them in oil at the beginning of making a curry.

Fennel seeds. Fennel is an annual plant; its dried seeds are light green and have a slight lico-

rice taste. When lightly roasted they taste sweeter. Chewing fennel seeds freshens the breath.

Fenugreek. Both the leaves and the seeds of this small annual herb can be used. The dried leaves are usually referred to as *methi*. The seeds are brown and hard and can be bitter; they are best used sparingly. The bitterness can become overpowering, especially with roasting; be careful not to overroast.

Garam masala is a blend or mixture of many different spices. The ingredients can vary depending on personal choice and what is available. (See my recipes for several different kinds of garam masala following this

CUMIN SEEDS

MUSTARD SEEDS

SPANISH PAPRIKA

section.) Although store-bought spice blends are available, the quality of homemade garam masala is always much better.

Ginger. Gingerroot is a rhizome (part of the root system of a flower). It is very aromatic and its flavor is sweet, spicy, and warm. Ground ginger is made from the dried rhizomes.

Mustard seeds. The mustard plant is an herb. The seeds are small and round and can be brown, black, yellow, or white. Lightly roasting them enhances their flavor.

Peppercorns. Black pepper is the dried unripe berry of a variety of tropical climbing vine. Ground peppercorns add pleasant heat and flavor.

Spanish paprika. A red powder produced from dried, finely ground pods and seeds of sweet peppers grown in Spain. Paprika can vary in sweetness and heat depending on the percentage of seeds in the peppers.

Turmeric is a tropical plant with a deep-yellow rhizome similar in appearance to ginger root. The rhizomes are boiled, dried, and ground into a bright-yellow powder. Turmeric gives a pleasant flavor and nice color to food. Be careful, though, as it does stain. It is sometimes used as a substitute for saffron for its yellow color.

TURMERIC

MY GARAM MASALA RECIPES

Garam masala is a mixture of the basic spices we used daily in my village. In India, there are many variations on garam masala: my aunts, who lived in different villages, each had their own masala mixes. Next I have given the recipe for my basic garam masala, and then, using that recipe as a base, I have provided three variations—all from the small villages of Punjab, India. You can use these homemade masalas in the many recipes in this book that call for them. Of course, you can always buy premade garam masala, but it's so simple to make your own, and the results are worth it.

It is important that you keep your garam masala fresh. If it has been in the pantry for more than three months, it's time to replace it!

Note about my recipes

If I do not specify "crushed" or "ground" in the recipes in this book, I'm referring to the whole seeds. This includes cumin, fennel, and mustard seeds. Sometimes I'll use a spice in ground and whole form in a single recipe.

My spices

Every time I give a cooking class, people want to know where I buy my spices. When I tell them I have them sent from the villages of India, I soon have a long list of requests for orders. This enthusiasm for fresh spices has inspired me to give back to my village and to provide people with spices of the best quality at the same time. My dream of starting a line of spices that originates in the villages of India has now become reality. I recently launched my own line of certified organic spices, which can be purchased from my website, www .balsworld.com. Part of the proceeds from the sales will go toward starting a foundation to support educational programs in my village. My project manager, Nathaniel Canuel, who has been involved with the Environmental Youth Alliance (EYA), will be supervising the project from the ground level. I am very excited about the opportunities that this foundation will offer for improving the lives of village women and children.

Which oil should you use?

Grapeseed oil contains unsaturated fat and essential fatty acids. It is believed to reduce LDL (the "bad" cholesterol) and raise HDL (the "good" cholesterol). It has a very light taste and can enhance the natural flavor of foods. It can be used in grilling, frying, salad dressings, and baking. It is high in antioxidants and can withstand a high cooking heat. *Olive oil* has a high content of monounsaturated fatty acids and antioxidant substances. Studies have shown it offers protection against heart disease by controlling LDL levels and raising HDL. It is also easy to digest. *Extra virgin olive oil*, which is oil from the first pressing extracted without the use of heat or solvents, has a lower acidity level and contains even higher levels of antioxidants. It is good for cooking and salad dressings. *Flaxseed oil* is rich in omega-3 and omega-6 essential fatty acids. It is excellent in salad dressings but should not be used for cooking or frying as heating the oil can alter its chemical composition.

GARAM MASALA
Makes about 1 cup (250 mL)

½ cup (125 mL) coriander seeds
½ cup (125 mL) cumin seeds
¼ cup (60 mL) black peppercorns
¼ cup (60 mL) curry leaves
3 whole cloves
2 black cardamom pods (kept whole)

2 cinnamon sticks, each 3 inches (8 cm) long
2 bay leaves

Preheat the oven to 325°F (160°C). Combine all the ingredients in a bowl and mix well. Spread the mixture on a rimmed baking sheet and toast in the oven for 15 minutes. Allow to cool, and remove the seeds from the cardamon pod, discarding the husk. Process the spice mixture to a fine powder in a grinder, such as a coffee grinder reserved for this purpose.

Store the garam masala in an airtight container in a cool place. It will keep well for 3 months.

8

TURMERIC MASALA
Makes about ½ cup (125 mL)

¼ cup (60 mL) ground coriander
2 Tbsp (30 mL) ground turmeric
1 Tbsp (15 mL) garam masala (page 7)
½ tsp (2 mL) salt
¼ tsp (1 mL) pepper

Combine all the ingredients in a bowl. Store in a glass jar with a tight-fitting lid.

GINGER MASALA
Makes about ½ cup (125 mL)

¼ cup (60 mL) ground cumin
2 Tbsp (30 mL) ground coriander
2 Tbsp (30 mL) ground ginger
1 Tbsp (15 mL) garam masala (page 7)
½ tsp (2 mL) salt
½ tsp (2 mL) pepper

Combine all the ingredients in a bowl. Store in a glass jar with a tight-fitting lid.

TANDOORI MASALA
Makes about ⅔ cup (160 mL)

¼ cup (60 mL) garam masala (page 7)
2 Tbsp (30 mL) ground coriander

2 Tbsp (30 mL) ground cumin
2 Tbsp (30 mL) Spanish paprika
½ tsp (2 mL) salt
½ tsp (2 mL) pepper

Combine all the ingredients in a bowl. Store in a glass jar with a tight-fitting lid.

OTHER INDIAN COOKING BASICS
How to make tamarind pulp

Tamarind is a dark brown fruit with sticky pulp containing seeds and fiber. It adds a pleasant sourness to dishes, and I often add a little bit of it to sauces and chutneys.

Tamarind (pulp and seeds) is sold pressed into small blocks, which are available in Indian grocery stores and often in the ethnic food section of supermarkets. Tamarind costs about two dollars for a package, so it's priced very reasonably and it can stay in the pantry for up to a year. I always have a block on hand.

However, you can't just cut off a chunk and add it to the recipe; you need to soak it and remove the seeds in order to make it useable. To do this, break off a chunk, about 2 Tbsp (30 mL), from the tamarind block. Place it in a bowl and add ¼ cup (60 mL) of hot water. Let it sit for at least 10 minutes. Then use a fork to separate the flavorful flesh from the seeds and fiber. Drain in a fine sieve over a bowl. Push the pulp through the sieve and discard the seeds and fiber. (I often use my hands to separate the seeds and fiber from the pulp.) Use the strained tamarind pulp and water, which should be like a purée, for cooking. This is what I am referring to when I call for tamarind pulp.

Because tamarind offers so many health benefits as an antioxidant and as a source of vitamins, minerals, and other nutrients, it is a definite must for your pantry.

How to make homemade paneer

Makes 2½ cups (625 mL),
about 1 lb (500 g)

Paneer is Punjabi cheese. Homemade paneer is always best, but you can also purchase it from an ethnic market. It is used in many recipes throughout the book, and is also delicious as an appetizer with chutney. I pan-fry the pieces and use it for cooking, or sometimes I grate or crumble it. It is so much fun to play with this cheese and create the dishes you desire.

8 cups (2 L) whole milk
4 cups (1 L) buttermilk

Bring the milk to a boil in a large pot. Add the buttermilk and stir until the mixture separates into solids and liquid. Line a sieve with cheesecloth and place it over a bowl. Pour the mixture into the cheesecloth-lined sieve to drain the curd, then discard the liquid.

Wrap the curd in the cheesecloth, place it in the sieve, and put a heavy weight, such as a cookie jar or rice container, on top. Let it drain for 20 minutes.

Remove the cheesecloth and cut the paneer into small cubes. Use immediately or refrigerate in a covered container for up to 5 days.

Pan-frying paneer

Pan-frying helps to keep the paneer from falling apart. Place 2 Tbsp (30 mL) of grapeseed oil in a nonstick pan over medium heat. When the oil is hot, gently place the paneer in the pan and cook until golden brown. Gently flip the pieces and brown the other side. Pan-fried paneer freezes and thaws very well without crumbling.

How to cook and freeze dried beans

I use a lot of beans in my recipes. Beans are high in protein and dietary fiber and low in fat, and they combine well with Indian spices in a variety of dishes.

You can use canned beans, but I prefer to use dried beans, in true Indian village style. In addition to being much cheaper, dried beans are much lower in sodium than canned beans. You can use any kind of dried beans, or a mixture of your favorite beans. Unlike other beans, lentils do not need to be soaked before cooking.

Rinse the beans and discard any stones. Place the beans in a pot and cover them with several inches (8 to 10 cm) of water, then cover the pot with a lid. Leave the beans to soak for at least 8 hours or overnight. Drain and rinse the beans, then cover them with fresh water. Bring to a boil, then cover and reduce the heat. Simmer until the beans are tender, about 45 minutes to 1½ hours. Drain the beans and let them cool.

Once the beans have cooled, they can be divided into small containers and frozen. When I want to make a salad or a curried

RICE FLAKES

bean dish, I just remember to thaw the beans by leaving them in the fridge overnight—just as convenient as opening a can.

(To substitute cooked dried beans for canned, note that a smaller can (14 oz or 398 mL) is the equivalent of about 1½ cups cooked beans; a larger can (19 oz or 540 mL) is about 2 cups.)

How to cook rice

I prefer to use brown rice as it is much higher in nutrients and dietary fiber than white rice. I love basmati brown rice because of its aroma, but I do use regular brown rice (long grain and short grain) on occasion as well.

I have only one trick to cook rice and it works every single time. I put rice in a saucepan. Then I rest the tip of my finger on the top of the dry rice and start adding water with my other hand. Once the water reaches the first knuckle of my finger, I stop adding the water. I place a lid on the saucepan and bring to a boil. Then I reduce the heat and let it simmer until the rice is cooked, about 40 minutes. (There is no need to let it sit.)

Rice flakes are another great item to have in your Indian pantry, ready to cook in minutes. See page 24 for instructions.

Salads

14

THE FIRST TIME I tried avocado was here in North America. I was intrigued by its creaminess, and I suspected it would go well with Indian spices and with chickpeas.

To grind cumin and cardamom, I use a coffee grinder reserved for this purpose. With cardamom, I remove the seeds from the pod and just use the seeds. I prefer green cardamom to black. *Serves 4*

Avocados are a good source of dietary fiber, health-promoting monounsaturated fats, vitamin C, and potassium (good for preventing muscle cramps). Once I learned all this I began using them on a regular basis in my cooking.

1. **To make the dressing**, combine the olive oil, lemon juice, ginger, cardamom, cumin, paprika, and salt in a small bowl and mix well.
2. Combine the avocados, chickpeas, and green onion in a large bowl and toss gently. Just before serving, pour the dressing over the salad and toss to thoroughly coat the ingredients.

Dressing

2 Tbsp (30 mL) olive oil

1 Tbsp (15 mL) lemon juice

1 Tbsp (15 mL) finely chopped ginger

½ tsp (2 mL) ground cardamom

¼ tsp (1 mL) ground cumin

⅛ tsp (0.5 mL) Spanish paprika

⅛ tsp (0.5 mL) salt

Salad

4 avocados, sliced

14 oz (398 mL) can chickpeas, drained and rinsed

¼ cup (60 mL) finely chopped green onion

IN MY VILLAGE we never had the convenience of canned beans. Dried lentils, chickpeas, and kidney beans were stored in huge sacks. When I was a child one of my jobs was to sort through a huge pile of beans and remove any small stones before my mother could cook with them.

Nowadays, I always have cans of various beans in my pantry. Also, I will sometimes make a big pot of beans and freeze some for later use (see page 10 for more on how to cook dried beans).

This recipe is very filling and great to take for lunches. The salad can be prepared in advance; in fact, the flavors meld together and intensify when the beans have had time to marinate. *Serves 4*

Beans are high in protein and are a major source of soluble fiber.

¼ cup (60 mL) finely chopped
    green onion
¼ cup (60 mL) finely chopped
    red onion
2 Tbsp (30 mL) lemon juice
2 Tbsp (30 mL) olive oil
½ tsp (2 mL) finely chopped garlic
½ tsp (2 mL) garam masala (page 7)
⅛ tsp (0.5 mL) Spanish paprika
salt to taste
14 oz (398 mL) can mixed beans,
    drained and rinsed

Combine the green onion, red onion, lemon juice, olive oil, garlic, garam masala, paprika, and salt in a large bowl. Stir until the oil and spices are well distributed. Add the mixed beans and stir until they are coated with the dressing. Refrigerate and serve cold.

BLACK BEAN AND COCONUT SALAD

I STILL REMEMBER the smell of fresh coconut from back home. The "coconut guy" would come to our village, and my brother would go out to the street to buy some as a treat for himself. I'd promise to iron my brother's clothes in return for a small piece of this special treat. Now, even though I can have all the fresh coconut I could ever want, it never seems to match the aroma and flavor of the fresh coconut of my past. *Serves 4*

Coconut is very rich in fiber and protein, so be good to yourself and indulge!

Toss all the ingredients together in a large bowl. Refrigerate and serve the salad chilled.

19 oz (540 mL) can black beans, drained and rinsed

¼ cup (60 mL) grated fresh coconut (sidebar page 100) or frozen shredded coconut

¼ cup (60 mL) finely chopped green onion

1 Tbsp (15 mL) finely chopped parsley

¼ tsp (1 mL) Ginger Masala (page 8)

¼ tsp (1 mL) ground cumin

¼ cup (60 mL) apple cider vinegar

1 Tbsp (15 mL) lime juice

2 Tbsp (30 mL) extra virgin olive oil

salt and pepper to taste

CHICKPEA AND KIDNEY BEAN SALAD WITH SESAME SEED DRESSING

THIS BEAN SALAD is totally delicious! I call for ground sesame seeds—I put ¼ cup (60 mL) of sesame seeds in a spice grinder or a coffee grinder to make approximately 2 Tbsp (30 mL) ground. Tahini (sesame paste), which can be purchased from your local grocery store, can also be used. *Serves 4*

Kidney beans are rich in fiber and high in iron. **Chickpeas** are high in protein and are a very good source of fiber, folate, and manganese. Kidney beans and chickpeas have other great health benefits: they are a source of carbohydrates and are very low on the glycemic index.

1. **To make the dressing**, combine all the ingredients in a small bowl and whisk together, adding the flaxseed oil last.
2. Combine all the salad ingredients in a large bowl. Add the dressing and toss until well combined. Refrigerate for an hour and serve chilled.

Sesame seed dressing

2 Tbsp (30 mL) ground sesame seeds (or tahini)
1 tsp (5 mL) finely chopped garlic
½ tsp (2 mL) ground fennel
½ tsp (2 mL) ground cardamom
salt and pepper to taste
¼ cup (60 mL) flaxseed oil

Salad

19 oz (540 mL) can kidney beans, drained and rinsed
19 oz (540 mL) can chickpeas, drained and rinsed
¼ cup (60 mL) finely diced red pepper
¼ cup (60 mL) finely diced yellow pepper
2 avocados, diced

CHICKPEA SALAD
WITH COCONUT DRESSING

THIS COCONUT DRESSING is enhanced by several aromatic spices. It's creamy, rich, and spicy, and will quickly transform simple ingredients like chickpeas and red pepper. *Serves 4*

What I love about **coconut** is that it is not only very flavorful but also highly nutritious and rich in vitamins and minerals. **Flaxseed oil** is rich in omega-3 and omega-6 essential fatty acids. This dressing is not just fragrant and delicious; it has the added attraction of being low in calories and high in nutrients and antioxidants.

1. **To make the dressing**, heat the grapeseed oil in a skillet over medium-high heat. When the oil is hot, add the mustard seeds, cumin seeds, coriander, and curry leaves and cook for 10 seconds. Add the coconut and reduce the heat to medium. Cook for 30 seconds, stirring regularly. Remove from the heat. Stir in the flaxseed oil and salt. Let the dressing cool before adding it to the salad.

2. Combine the chickpeas, red pepper, chives, and lemon juice in a large bowl. Add the coconut dressing and mix gently until the ingredients are evenly combined. Refrigerate and serve chilled.

Coconut dressing
1 Tbsp (15 mL) grapeseed oil
1 tsp (5 mL) mustard seeds
1 tsp (5 mL) cumin seeds
1 tsp (5 mL) ground coriander
6 curry leaves
¼ cup (60 mL) unsweetened dried coconut flakes
3 Tbsp (45 mL) flaxseed oil
salt to taste

[handwritten: ½ tsp curry]
[handwritten: 2 tbsp coconut]
[handwritten: 2 tbsp grapeseed]

Salad
14 oz (398 mL) can chickpeas, drained and rinsed
¼ cup (60 mL) finely chopped red pepper
¼ cup (60 mL) finely chopped chives
1 Tbsp (15 mL) lemon juice

[handwritten: 5.5 pts for 4 serving]

MY DEAR FRIEND Paul had never tasted Indian food until he met me. He now loves paneer, and loves this salad. When I showed him how to make this Indian cheese from scratch, he couldn't believe it could be done in less than half an hour (see page 10 for instructions). *Serves 4*

When Paul told me that **beets** contain several vitamins and minerals, I was inspired to do some research. Beets have been used for centuries as a medicinal treatment for a variety of conditions and have amazing health benefits. They are high in folate and antioxidants, and have been shown to prevent colon cancer and lower LDL (the "bad" cholesterol). That is one of the reasons I often prepare this salad for my family.

2 large beets, peeled and cut into
   bite-sized pieces
2 Tbsp (30 mL) grapeseed oil
1 tsp (5 mL) garam masala (page 7)
½ tsp (5 mL) coriander, crushed
10 to 12 curry leaves
salt and pepper to taste
¼ cup (60 mL) grated paneer
   (page 10)
1 tsp (5 mL) lime juice

1. **Place the beets** in a saucepan and add enough water to cover. Bring to a boil, then reduce the heat to medium and cook for 8 to 10 minutes, or until the beets are still slightly crunchy. Remove from the heat, drain, and cool slightly.

2. Heat the oil in a skillet over medium-high heat. When the oil is hot, add the garam masala, coriander, and curry leaves and cook for 5 seconds. Add the salt, pepper, and grated paneer and cook until the paneer turns golden brown, about 15 to 20 seconds. Turn the heat off and add the lime juice.

3. Sprinkle the paneer mixture over the beets and toss before serving. Serve warm.

IN THE VILLAGE, picking fresh olives was very common, and we ate them with salads or as sides. I'd slice them thinly and place them in the middle of my roti. While men were allowed to eat their food however they wanted to, women were supposed to eat their roti daintily, one bite-sized piece at a time. So of course it was frowned upon by my female elders whenever I'd eat my olive roti as a wrap!

We had only one kind of olive—simple green ones—so I love living in North America, where a quick trip to the grocery store gives me access to such a great variety. For this recipe I do use green olives, but try any kind you like. *Serves 4*

Olives are high in monounsaturated fats and a good source of vitamin E, iron, copper, and fiber.

2 large beets, peeled and cut into bite-sized pieces

1 cup (250 mL) pitted and sliced green olives

¼ cup (60 mL) chopped cilantro

¼ cup (60 mL) finely chopped red onion

3 Tbsp (45 mL) flaxseed oil

1 Tbsp (15 mL) lemon juice

1 Tbsp (15 mL) fennel seeds

salt to taste

1. **Place the beets** in a saucepan and add enough water to cover. Bring the water to a boil, then reduce the heat to medium and cook for 10 to 12 minutes, or until the beets are still slightly crunchy. Remove from the heat, drain, and cool slightly.

2. Place the beets in a large bowl. Add the remaining ingredients and stir to combine thoroughly. Refrigerate for at least 2 hours and serve chilled.

CARROT AND APPLE SALAD

WHERE I GREW up, apples weren't grown locally and were expensive—half a delicious slice was considered a real treat. Since they were such a luxury, apples were not mixed with anything, and definitely not with carrots. Carrots were just an everyday vegetable that grew like a weed in the garden. I think I've made a lovely treat here, though, daring to have combined the two! *Serves 4*

Apples are a good source of fiber and vitamin C.

Combine all the ingredients in a large bowl and mix well. Refrigerate the salad for at least 2 hours and serve it chilled.

2 cups (500 mL) peeled and thinly sliced carrots

2 cups (500 mL) peeled and chopped apples

¼ cup (60 mL) red wine vinegar

1 Tbsp (15 mL) fennel seeds

½ tsp (2 mL) ground cardamom

¼ tsp (1 mL) ground coriander

salt and pepper to taste

WE WEREN'T ALLOWED to associate with lower-caste people or share food or drink with them—the caste system was well in effect in the village. Despite this, I did make friends with a girl named Kuldeep. We would meet secretly to exchange food, and on many occasions she brought me rice-flake snacks. Now, whenever I cook with rice flakes, I think of Kuldeep, whom I miss very much.

Rice flakes are made by boiling rice and then pounding it into flakes. Most North Americans are not familiar with this inexpensive, versatile, and low-calorie carbohydrate, which can be purchased from any Indian grocery store. To cook, simply put the rice flakes in a strainer and run them under hot water for 10 seconds, then under cold water for 5 seconds. Fluff them with a fork—ready in an instant! *Serves 4*

2 Tbsp (30 mL) grapeseed oil
1 Tbsp (15 mL) cumin seeds
1 tsp (5 mL) mustard seeds
1 tsp (5 mL) ground cardamom
1 cup (250 mL) shelled edamame, cooked (see instructions below)
2 cups (500 mL) cooked rice flakes (see instructions in recipe intro)
¼ cup (60 mL) finely chopped green onion
½ tsp (2 mL) Spanish paprika
salt and pepper to taste
1 Tbsp (15 mL) lime juice
1 cup (250 mL) thinly sliced red radishes (optional)

1. **Heat the oil** in a skillet over medium-high heat. When the oil is hot, add the cumin seeds, mustard seeds, and cardamom and cook for 20 seconds. Add the edamame and cook for 1 minute. Stir in the rice flakes, green onion, paprika, salt, and pepper and cook for 2 minutes. Turn the heat off and allow the mixture to cool.

2. Add the lime juice and radishes (if using) to the skillet and stir well. Serve warm or at room temperature.

How to cook edamame
Place 1 cup (250 mL) of frozen or fresh shelled edamame and 2 cups (500 mL) of water in a medium saucepan and bring to a boil. Reduce the heat to low and cook for 3 to 5 minutes. Drain the beans and set them aside to cool.

SIMPLE TURNIP SALAD
WITH RASPBERRY DRESSING

I GREW UP eating raw turnip (*shalgams*) from the garden. I still include raw turnip in my cold salads, and its tangy smell takes me right back to the village.

I think that tomatoes and cucumbers complement turnips beautifully, and the mint in the dressing makes everything even more refreshing. My mother always used mint to make chutneys. I couldn't have been any older than five when I grew my very own mint plant in the village garden. *Serves 4*

I hope you like the combination of **raspberries** and **mint** as much as I do—especially when I tell you that mint is a powerful antioxidant and is rich in vitamins A, C, and B12, thiamine, folate, and riboflavin. And raspberries are loaded with vitamins, antioxidants, and fiber. Eating this salad is good for your health!

1. **To make the dressing**, combine all the ingredients in a blender and process until the mint is finely chopped.
2. Place all the salad ingredients in a large bowl; toss to combine. Drizzle the dressing over the salad and mix it well just before serving.
3. Serve chilled.

Raspberry dressing

½ cup (125 mL) fresh
    or frozen raspberries
¼ cup (60 mL) loosely packed
    mint leaves
2 Tbsp (30 mL) balsamic vinegar
2 Tbsp (30 mL) liquid honey
¼ tsp (1 mL) garam masala (page 7)
⅛ tsp (0.5 mL) Spanish paprika
⅛ tsp (0.5 mL) salt
¼ cup (60 mL) flaxseed oil

Salad

4 large tomatoes, seeded and sliced
2 large cucumbers, thinly sliced
2 cups (500 mL) peeled and finely
    chopped turnip

FRESH SUMMER CUCUMBER SALAD WITH YOGURT DRESSING

I WAS RUNNING late to work and decided to put together a quick summer salad for my lunch by using whatever ingredients I could find in the fridge—it was a bit of a surprise how good it turned out to be. My daughter loved it too and made sure I wrote down the recipe.

This salad was inspired by *raita*, a cooling side dish made with yogurt. I love raita, and it was fun adding other flavors to raita ingredients. *Serves 4*

I love using **cilantro**, not only for its fresh flavor, but also because it's nutritious—it's a source of iron and magnesium and contains immunity-boosting properties.

1. **To make the dressing**, combine all the ingredients in a small bowl. Whisk them together until thoroughly combined.
2. Combine all the salad ingredients in a large bowl. Add the dressing, toss well, and serve at room temperature.

Yogurt dressing

½ cup (125 mL) plain yogurt
¼ tsp (1 mL) garam masala (page 7)
¼ tsp (1 mL) ground cardamom
salt and pepper to taste

Salad

1 large cucumber, finely chopped
1 cup (250 mL) frozen or fresh peas
¼ cup (60 mL) finely chopped
   red onion
2 Tbsp (30 mL) finely
   chopped cilantro
1 tsp (5 mL) fennel seeds

IN THE VILLAGE we had something very similar to capers, called *kair* (aka *Capparis decidua*). They were grown on a large bush, and I would collect each tiny piece and sprinkle sugar on them before eating.

Capers were my starting point for this refreshing, light salad. The strong, salty capers balance the sharp flavor of red onion and the coolness of cucumber, and the fig dressing is sweet and spicy. *Serves 4*

I was surprised to learn that **capers** are a relatively good source of fiber and iron. **Figs** are high in natural and simple sugars and fiber. They also contain good levels of minerals such as potassium, calcium, and iron—who knew?

1. **To make the dressing**, combine all the ingredients in a food processor and process until the figs are fully puréed.
2. Combine all the salad ingredients in a large bowl. Pour the dressing over the salad and toss. Serve at room temperature.

Fig dressing

4 medium dried figs
¼ cup (60 mL) flaxseed oil
1 Tbsp (15 mL) liquid honey
¼ tsp (1 mL) ground cardamom
¼ tsp (1 mL) ground fennel
¼ tsp (1 mL) ground cumin
salt and pepper to taste

Salad

2 cups (500 mL) cherry tomatoes
1 large cucumber, chopped
¼ cup (60 mL) finely chopped red onion
1 Tbsp (15 mL) capers

WHITE RADISH SALAD
WITH CHERRY DRESSING

IN THE VILLAGE during winter, white radish (*mooli*, also known as *daikon*) would traditionally be eaten raw in a cold salad. It was a very simple but very flavorful salad. Here I've made something similar to what we used to eat, but I've added cucumber, cherries, and ginger. The sweet, warm flavors of the spices contrast with the cool crunch of white radish. *Serves 4*

I've come to appreciate **radishes** as they are rich in vitamin C and have detoxifying properties. The cherry dressing is light and healthy. **Cherries** contain high levels of antioxidants as well as important nutrients such as beta-carotene, vitamin C, potassium, magnesium, iron, fiber, and folate.

Cherry dressing

½ cup (125 mL) canned or fresh
   pitted cherries
¼ cup (60 mL) flaxseed oil
1 Tbsp (15 mL) lime juice
½ tsp (2 mL) Ginger Masala (page 8)
¼ tsp (1 mL) Spanish paprika
salt and pepper to taste

Salad

2 cups (500 mL) thinly sliced
   white radish
1 cucumber, thinly sliced
1 tsp (5 mL) freshly grated ginger

1. **To make the dressing**, combine all the ingredients in a large bowl. Using a food processor or a blender, process or blend until the cherries are completely puréed.
2. Combine the radish, cucumber, and ginger in a large bowl. Drizzle the dressing over the salad and toss well before serving.

30

I WAS NOT at all familiar with the luscious green spears of asparagus until I came to North America. I was struck by its crisp texture and nutty flavor, and have been cooking asparagus regularly ever since. *Serves 4*

Radishes and **asparagus** are both rich sources of vitamin C, vitamin A, fiber, and protein.

1. **Heat the oil** in a skillet over medium-high heat. When the oil is hot, add the garlic, coriander seeds, cumin seeds, and salt. Cook for 10 seconds. Add the asparagus and cook for 2 minutes. Sprinkle the sesame seeds overtop and cook for 10 more seconds. Sprinkle with the lemon juice and turn the heat off. Add the radish to the skillet.

2. Serve the salad warm, with the juices remaining in the pan drizzled overtop.

1 Tbsp (15 mL) grapeseed oil

1 tsp (5 mL) finely chopped garlic

1 Tbsp (15 mL) coriander seeds, crushed

1 tsp (5 mL) cumin seeds

pinch salt

1 lb (500 g) asparagus, ends snapped off and spears cut into bite-sized pieces

1 Tbsp (15 mL) sesame seeds

1 Tbsp (15 mL) lemon juice

1 cup (250 mL) julienned white radish (*mooli*, aka *daikon*)

32

I GREW UP eating raw vegetables every day, and I still love them for their crunch, freshness, and flavor. I was having some friends over to watch the *Sex and the City* movie, and I wanted to make something attractive, delicious, and nutritious. (Of course I try to do this with all of my recipes!) Not only did the radish and kiwi look great with their contrasting red and green, they also tasted great. And I've always found that cumin and coriander (the main ingredients in my garam masala) have a richness that balances beautifully with raw veggies. *Serves 4*

Kiwifruit are rich in many vitamins, particularly vitamin C. They are also a good source of potassium and beta-carotene.

1. **For the chicken**, combine the garam masala, paprika, and salt in a small bowl and mix well. Place the chicken breast halves on a plate and sprinkle the spice mixture on both sides of each half.

2. Heat the oil in a skillet over medium-high heat. When the oil is hot, gently place the chicken in the skillet and cook for about 12 to 15 minutes, turning frequently to make sure all sides are cooked and golden brown. The chicken should be white all the way through when tested. Set the chicken aside to cool, then cut it into bite-sized pieces.

3. Combine all the salad ingredients in a large bowl. Add the chicken. Gently mix everything together and refrigerate for 2 hours. Serve chilled.

Chicken

1 Tbsp (15 mL) garam masala
   (page 7)
1 tsp (5 mL) Spanish paprika
salt to taste
2 boneless, skinless chicken breasts,
   each cut in half
2 Tbsp (30 mL) grapeseed oil

Salad

1 cup (250 mL) thinly sliced
   red radishes
1 cup (250 mL) thinly sliced
   white radish (*mooli*, aka *daikon*)
1 cup (250 mL) peeled and thinly
   sliced kiwi
2 Tbsp (30 mL) flaxseed oil
1 Tbsp (15 mL) lime juice
½ tsp (2 mL) ground cardamom
salt and pepper to taste

I LOVE THE flavor of fennel seeds, and even when they are added to other spices, fennel's warm, distinct, licorice-like flavor can still be appreciated. In the village we ate fennel seeds at the end of the meal to freshen our breath. We also used them in chai tea. *Serves 4*

Fennel seeds are good for the digestive system. They are also rich in iron, calcium, and vitamin C.

1. **Prepare the pearl barley** by combining the water, barley, garam masala, and salt in a pot over medium-high heat and bringing it to a boil. Reduce the heat to low, cover the pot, and cook until the water is fully absorbed and the barley has fluffed up, about 10 minutes. Remove from the heat and allow to cool.

2. While the barley is cooking, prepare the chicken. Heat the oil in a skillet over medium-high heat. When the oil is hot, add the shallots, cashews, fennel seeds, cumin seeds, Turmeric Masala, salt, and pepper and cook for 30 seconds. Lower the heat to medium and add the chicken. Sauté, stirring regularly, until the chicken is cooked through, about 7 to 9 minutes.

3. Add the cooled barley to the chicken mixture and combine well. Cover and refrigerate for about 1 hour, until chilled. Sprinkle with the fresh lime juice just before serving.

Barley

2 cups (500 mL) water

1 cup (250 mL) pearl barley

1 tsp (5 mL) garam masala (page 7)

salt to taste

Chicken

2 Tbsp (30 mL) grapeseed oil

¼ cup (60 mL) finely
    chopped shallots

¼ cup (60 mL) cashews

1 Tbsp (15 mL) fennel seeds

1 tsp (5 mL) cumin seeds

½ tsp (2 mL) Turmeric Masala
    (page 8)

salt and pepper to taste

1 lb (500 g) boneless, skinless
    chicken breasts, cut into
    bite-sized pieces

1 Tbsp (15 mL) lime juice

Starters

SPICY REFRIED BEAN DIP

THE FIRST TIME I ate nachos with refried beans I knew immediately that I would have to try them with my own spices, and I created this recipe that very same night. Coriander, cumin, and turmeric go very well with the beans. Trust me—after making this you will never want to eat plain (dare I say *bland!*) refried beans again.
Serves 4

2 Tbsp (30 mL) grapeseed oil

1 medium red onion, finely chopped

1 Tbsp (15 mL) finely chopped garlic

1 Tbsp (15 mL) cumin seeds

1 tsp (5 mL) ground coriander

¼ tsp (1 mL) ground turmeric

½ tsp (2 mL) salt

¼ cup (60 mL) finely chopped
   green onion

1 cup (250 mL) finely
   chopped tomatoes

14 oz (398 mL) can refried beans

¼ cup (60 mL) water

1 Tbsp (15 mL) lemon juice

1. **Heat the oil** in a skillet over medium-high heat. When the oil is hot, add the onion, garlic, and cumin seeds and cook for 2 minutes, stirring regularly. Stir in the coriander, turmeric, salt, green onion, and tomatoes. Cook for 2 minutes. Add the refried beans and water, reduce the heat to medium-low, and cook for 3 minutes. Turn the heat off and stir in the lemon juice.

2. Serve warm with nachos or chips. Enjoy!

BAKED BUTTERNUT SQUASH DIP

I OFTEN COOK squash in the traditional village style—on a stovetop, with onion and ginger. But once I had access to an oven, I was inspired to do something different with this vegetable. So I made a dip! Fennel seeds and ginger are perfect with butternut squash. *Makes 1½ cups (375 mL)*

It's great to have lots of ways in which to prepare **squash** since it is a very good source of vitamin C, potassium, and fiber.

1 butternut squash, about 2 lb (1 kg)
1 Tbsp (15 mL) grapeseed oil
2 Tbsp (30 mL) fennel seeds
1 Tbsp (15 mL) freshly grated ginger
1 tsp (5 mL) ground cardamom
salt and pepper to taste

1. **Preheat the oven** to 400°F (200°C). Cut the squash in half; remove and discard all the seeds. Brush the insides of the squash halves with the oil and place them on a baking sheet with the cut sides up. Combine the fennel seeds, ginger, cardamom, salt, and pepper in a small bowl and sprinkle over the squash.
2. Place the baking sheet on the middle rack of the oven and bake for 1 hour and 20 minutes. Remove from the oven and allow the squash to cool.
3. Scoop the flesh from the shells and place it in a bowl. Stir well so the spices are mixed in thoroughly. Serve warm with crackers or chips.

40

THIS RECIPE IS inspired by those students of mine who love vegetarian dishes. I dedicate it to all the vegetarians and wannabe-vegetarians, like my son, Aaron. *Serves 4*

Zucchini adds important nutrients to this recipe—it contains vitamin C and lutein, which promotes eye health.

1. **Heat the oil** in a skillet over medium-high heat. When the oil is hot, add the ginger and cumin seeds, reduce the heat to low to medium, and cook for 10 seconds. Stir in the zucchini, mushrooms, garam masala, paprika, and salt. Cook for 5 to 7 minutes.

2. Place a tortilla in a large skillet over low to medium heat. Spread half of the vegetable mixture over the tortilla, leaving a clear margin around the outside edge so the filling doesn't spill out. Sprinkle ¼ cup (60 mL) of the cheese on top of the mixture and cover with another tortilla. As soon as the cheese begins to melt and the first tortilla is nicely browned, flip the whole quesadilla with a spatula and brown the second tortilla. Transfer to a cutting board and cut into wedges with a pizza cutter. Repeat with the remaining ingredients.

3. Serve with a mint or a cilantro chutney.

2 Tbsp (30 mL) grapeseed oil

2 Tbsp (30 mL) freshly grated ginger

1 tsp (5 mL) cumin seeds

1 medium zucchini, thinly sliced

2 medium portobello mushrooms, thinly sliced

1 Tbsp (15 mL) garam masala (page 7)

¼ tsp (1 mL) Spanish paprika

¼ tsp (1 mL) salt

4 large soft flour tortillas

½ cup (125 mL) shredded mozzarella cheese

SPICED-HONEY CHICKEN ON GARLIC ASPARAGUS

THIS IS A great appetizer to serve at a dinner party. When I first made it for my friends, they all wanted the recipe, saying it would be a great lunch item for their children; and indeed, it was an immediate hit with my seven-year-old. Serve it with any one of my chutneys.

Serves 4

2 Tbsp (30 mL) grapeseed oil
¼ cup (60 mL) finely chopped red onion
1 Tbsp (15 mL) finely chopped ginger
1 lb (500 g) boneless, skinless chicken breasts, cut into bite-sized pieces
¼ cup (60 mL) honey
1 Tbsp (15 mL) ground coriander
1 tsp (5 mL) Tandoori Masala (page 8)
1 tsp (5 mL) ground cardamom
salt and pepper to taste

1. **Heat the oil** in a skillet over medium heat. When the oil is hot, add the onion and ginger and cook for 2 minutes, stirring regularly. Add the chicken pieces and sauté, stirring frequently, until almost cooked through, about 5 minutes.
2. Add the honey, coriander, Tandoori Masala, cardamom, salt, and pepper to the skillet and stir well. Cook until the chicken is nicely glazed with the honey mixture, about 7 minutes.
3. Serve over a bed of Garlic Asparagus.

GARLIC ASPARAGUS

I CREATED THIS side dish or appetizer because my son doesn't like steamed asparagus. Since asparagus is so healthy, I decided to sauté the asparagus, with the addition of a few spices. It was a great hit! The garlic and coriander balances the sharpness of asparagus. Trust me, you will love this recipe.

2 Tbsp (30 mL) grapeseed oil
1 Tbsp (15 mL) finely chopped garlic
1 Tbsp (15 mL) coriander seeds, crushed
1 lb (500 g) asparagus, ends snapped off
salt and pepper to taste
2 Tbsp (30 mL) water

Heat the oil in a small skillet over medium-high heat. When the oil is hot, add the garlic and coriander seeds and cook for 10 seconds. Add the asparagus, salt, and pepper and cook for 2 minutes, stirring frequently. Add the water and cook for another minute before serving.

42

THESE DON'T TAKE long to put together, and they're really popular with my kids and their friends. When my six-year-old son has his friends over for a playdate, this is all they seem to want. They like to help make them, too. I've offered to teach my 17-year-old daughter and her friends how to prepare this themselves, but so far they only seem interested in eating! *Serves 4*

I love adding dried **fenugreek leaves** to my recipes for their distinct aroma and also for the added benefits of protein, vitamin C, niacin, and potassium.

1 lb (500 g) boneless, skinless
chicken breasts
¾ cup (185 mL) plain low-fat yogurt
½ cup (125 mL) chickpea flour
2 Tbsp (30 mL) dried
fenugreek leaves
1½ Tbsp (22.5 mL) garam masala
(page 7)
1 tsp (5 mL) Spanish paprika
salt and pepper to taste
2 Tbsp (30 mL) grapeseed oil

1. **Cut the chicken breasts** into long strips about 1 inch (2.5 cm) wide. Combine the yogurt, chickpea flour, fenugreek (crushing it with your hands as you add it), garam masala, paprika, salt, and pepper in a bowl. Stir well. Add the chicken strips and coat well with the mixture.
2. Heat the oil in a nonstick skillet over medium-high heat. When the oil is hot, carefully place the coated chicken in the skillet and reduce the heat to medium. Cook until the chicken is done, about 8 to 10 minutes, turning the strips frequently so all sides are nicely browned. The meat should be white all the way through and should pull apart easily.
3. Serve with Mint and Mango Chutney (see next).

continued

Masala Chicken Fingers (continued)

MINT AND MANGO CHUTNEY
Makes about 1 cup (250 mL)

MANGOES ARE DELICIOUS when ripe and in season. During the off-season, I use canned mango pulp, which is available in ethnic stores. This refreshing and flavorful chutney takes only seconds to prepare.

Place all the ingredients in a food processor and process until smooth. Keep in a covered glass container for up to 5 days in the refrigerator.

2 cups (500 mL) ripe mango chunks OR 1 cup (250 mL) canned mango pulp

1 cup (250 mL) loosely packed mint leaves

½ cup (125 mL) chopped red onion

1 medium green chili, finely chopped (optional)

1 Tbsp (15 mL) lemon juice

1 tsp (5 mL) garam masala (page 7)

1 tsp (5 mL) ground coriander

salt and pepper to taste

¼ cup (60 mL) water

BARBECUED INDIAN CHICKEN WINGS

MY MOTHER COOKED on an open barbecue pit, but those who lived in cities had portable barbecues called *tandoors*. Relatives who lived in the city brought their tandoors when they came back to visit for special occasions, which was also when meat dishes, such as chicken and goat, were cooked. If I ever had to cook chicken wings in the village again, this is the recipe I would use.

Serves 4

2 cups (500 mL) plain yogurt
¼ cup (60 mL) tomato paste
1 Tbsp (15 mL) finely chopped garlic
¼ cup (60 mL) dried
    fenugreek leaves
2 Tbsp (30 mL) garam masala
    (page 7)
1 Tbsp (15 mL) brown sugar
1 tsp (5 mL) ground cardamom
1 tsp (5 mL) cayenne pepper
salt to taste
20 chicken wings (aka drummettes)

1. **Combine all the ingredients** except the chicken wings in a large bowl and mix well. Set aside ¼ cup (60 mL) of the marinade for basting. Add the chicken wings to the remaining marinade in the bowl, cover, and marinate for at least 45 minutes or up to 4 hours in the refrigerator.
2. Preheat the barbecue to medium-high heat.
3. Remove the chicken wings from the marinade and place them on the grill. Reduce the heat to medium. Grill, basting regularly with the reserved marinade and turning frequently to make sure that all sides are nicely cooked, for about 20 to 30 minutes.
4. Serve with any sauce you like for dipping; I love to serve these wings with a sweet-and-sour sauce.

WHAT I REALLY love about this recipe is that you don't have to marinate the chicken for too long since the mint (in the marinade) is so strong. I created this when Brad Frenette requested recipes for his *National Post* column, "The Appetizer." I got a lot of great feedback for this recipe, and it's now often on my menu when I am entertaining friends. *Serves 4*

Mint is very refreshing, contains vitamins A, C, and B12, and is a good source of antioxidants.

1. **In a large bowl**, combine the mint, tamarind pulp, oil, ginger, garam masala, brown sugar, and salt and mix well. Stir in the chicken. Cover the bowl and marinate in the refrigerator for at least 30 minutes or up to 2 hours.
2. Preheat the barbecue to medium heat. (If using wooden skewers, soak them in water for 30 minutes before using.)
3. Thread the chicken onto skewers. Grill the kabobs on the preheated barbecue for 15 to 20 minutes, turning frequently to make sure all sides are cooked through.
4. Serve with Spicy Raita (see next).

½ cup (125 mL) finely chopped mint
2 Tbsp (30 mL) tamarind pulp (page 8)
2 Tbsp (30 mL) grapeseed oil
1 Tbsp (15 mL) freshly grated ginger
1 Tbsp (15 mL) garam masala (page 7)
1 Tbsp (15 mL) brown sugar
salt to taste
1 lb (500 g) boneless, skinless chicken breasts, cut into 1½-inch (4 cm) pieces
6 metal or wooden skewers

Suggested wine

2009 *Pinot Blanc by Lake Breeze Vineyards* | This wine is all about fruit flavors and aromas. Its clean, crisp, and ever-so-slightly sweet/sour finish works beautifully with the mint and grainy mustard in my recipe.

continued

Mint and Ginger Chicken Kabobs (continued)

SPICY RAITA

Makes about 1 cup (250 mL)

THIS DIP CAN be made ahead of time and it will keep
well in the refrigerator for three to four days.

Combine all the ingredients in a small serving bowl
and stir until well mixed.

1 cup (250 mL) plain low-fat yogurt
1 Tbsp (15 mL) chopped mint
1 Tbsp (15 mL) finely
   chopped chives
1 Tbsp (15 mL) lemon juice
1 tsp (5 mL) prepared grainy mustard
salt and pepper to taste

MINI BUFFALO BURGER PATTIES

WHENEVER I SEE buffalo meat now at the store or market, it always makes me think of the water buffalo in India (despite the fact that it's a different animal from the American buffalo sold as meat here). I would see the water buffalo wandering in the streets, and I'd always be scared of them, but the female elders would feed them plain dough as it was believed that would bring wealth to the household. I was surprised to see that the buffalo I had known in India were quite different animals from the ones in North America.

Since buffalo meat is very lean, I've added mango sauce for moisture. The sweetness of mango goes very well with the spices. *Serves 4*

Buffalo (aka bison) meat has more protein, fewer calories, and less fat than other red meat. Now I regularly have it on the menu.

1 lb (500 g) minced buffalo
   (bison) meat
½ cup (125 mL) dried breadcrumbs
¼ cup (60 mL) finely chopped
   ripe mango
1 Tbsp (15 mL) freshly grated ginger
1 Tbsp (15 mL) fennel seeds
1 Tbsp (15 mL) ground cumin
1 tsp (5 mL) Turmeric Masala
   (page 8)
salt to taste

1. **Preheat the barbecue** to medium-high heat.
2. In a large bowl, stir together all the ingredients, mixing until evenly combined. Form the mixture into 2-inch (5 cm) patties. Reduce the barbecue heat to medium and gently place the patties on the grill. Cook for about 9 to 12 minutes, turning frequently to make sure both sides are browned.
3. Serve the burgers with a desired sauce or chutney. My son loves them with ketchup.

50

ANOOP LOVES PRAWNS, so I made this appetizer when her friends came for a sleepover. It was such a hit with the girls that they literally licked up the last of the roasted garlic and fennel dip! It always feels good to serve something not only delicious but healthy too. *Serves 4*

I like using **garlic** in my dishes because it contains *allicin*, which is known to have antibacterial, antiviral, antifungal, and antioxidant properties. Garlic and fennel go very well together.

1. **To make the dip**, heat the oil in a skillet over medium-low heat. Add the garlic cloves and cook for 5 minutes, stirring regularly. Remove from the heat. When the garlic is cool, remove the skins and mash the flesh with a fork.

2. In a medium bowl, combine the mashed garlic, sour cream, oil, ground fennel, salt, and paprika. Whisk the mixture until it is thoroughly combined. Refrigerate.

3. To make the prawns, thoroughly combine the yogurt, garam masala, fennel seeds, cardamom, paprika, and salt in a large bowl. Add the prawns and stir to coat them well with the mixture. Cover and refrigerate for 20 minutes.

4. Preheat the barbecue to medium heat. (If using wooden skewers, soak them in water for 30 minutes before using.)

5. Thread one prawn onto each skewer. Gently place the skewers on the preheated grill, turning frequently until the prawns are cooked, about 3 minutes.

6. Serve with lime wedges and the Garlic-Fennel Dip.

Garlic-fennel dip

1 Tbsp (15 mL) grapeseed oil
10 garlic cloves, unpeeled
¼ cup (60 mL) sour cream
2 Tbsp (30 mL) flaxseed oil
1 tsp (5 mL) ground fennel
pinch salt
pinch Spanish paprika

Prawns

¼ cup (60 mL) plain low-fat yogurt
1 Tbsp (15 mL) garam masala
  (page 7)
1 tsp (5 mL) fennel seeds, ground
  or kept whole
1 tsp (5 mL) ground cardamom
1 tsp (5 mL) Spanish paprika
salt to taste
18 large raw prawns, heads removed,
  shelled, and deveined
18 metal or wooden skewers
6 lime wedges

Suggested wine

2006 Syrah by Nichol Vineyard
This wine has aromas of cherry and plum, and hints of roasted meat, with flavors of bright cherry and black pepper. Its velvety-soft finish pairs well with the fennel, cardamom, and Spanish paprika in this recipe.

AT OUR HOUSE no party is complete unless I serve these quick, flavorful, and delicious prawns. They're the perfect finger food, so simple and easy to make. *Serves 4*

1. **Heat the oil** in a skillet over medium-high heat. When the oil is hot, reduce the heat to medium. Add the garlic and cook for 10 seconds. Add the coriander seeds, cumin seeds, and fenugreek leaves and cook for another 10 seconds.

2. Stir in the prawns and reduce the heat to medium. Sauté, stirring frequently, until they are fully cooked, about 3 to 5 minutes. Add the sesame seeds, salt, and pepper and cook for 10 more seconds.

3. Remove from the heat, sprinkle with the lime juice, and serve immediately with any sauce or chutney.

2 Tbsp (30 mL) grapeseed oil
1 Tbsp (15 mL) finely chopped garlic
1 Tbsp (15 mL) coriander seeds, crushed
1 Tbsp (15 mL) cumin seeds
1 Tbsp (15 mL) dried fenugreek leaves, crushed
20 large raw prawns, heads removed, shelled, and deveined
1 Tbsp (15 mL) sesame seeds
salt and pepper to taste
1 Tbsp (15 mL) lime juice

EGGPLANT AND MANGO DIP

I NEVER WOULD have thought of using eggplant in a dip, but then I saw some recipes when I moved to Canada. I came up with this when I was experimenting with eggplant, and it's now a favorite of my kids. *Serves 4*

Eggplant is an excellent source of fiber, and because mangoes are rich in vitamin A (beta-carotene) and antioxidants, this is a healthy combination.

3 Tbsp (45 mL) grapeseed oil
1 Tbsp (15 mL) garam masala (page 7)
1 tsp (5 mL) Ginger Masala (page 8)
½ tsp (2 mL) ground turmeric
½ tsp (2 mL) fenugreek seeds
salt and pepper to taste
1 medium eggplant, peeled and finely chopped
1 large mango, peeled, pitted, and mashed with a fork

1. **Heat the oil** in a skillet over medium-high heat. Once the oil is hot, reduce the heat to medium and add the garam masala, Ginger Masala, turmeric, fenugreek seeds, salt, and pepper. Cook for about 5 seconds. Add the eggplant and cook until it is soft, about 9 to 12 minutes, stirring regularly.
2. Add the mango to the skillet and cook for another 2 minutes, stirring to combine well.
3. Serve warm with tortilla chips.

54

NOT ONLY IS this dish beautiful with its dark green and rich red colors, but it also features a delicious blend of spices: fennel and cardamom. It's a perfect accompaniment to seafood. We never had beets growing up in the village, so I definitely feel like I've been missing out! I make this recipe a lot to make up for it. *Serves 4*

Beets are a good source of fiber, vitamin C, magnesium, iron, copper, and phosphorus. Add beets to **spinach** and you get twice the health benefits, as spinach is also rich in vitamin C and fiber and contains other nutrients, such as calcium, folate, vitamin K, and iron.

1. **Place the beets** and water in a large saucepan over high heat. Bring to a boil, then cover the saucepan and reduce the heat to low. Simmer until the beets are cooked, about 7 to 10 minutes. Drain the beets and let them cool, then slice them thinly.

2. Heat the oil in a skillet over medium-high heat. When the oil is hot, add the fenugreek leaves, fennel seeds, cardamom, salt, and pepper and cook for 5 to 7 seconds. Add the beets and stir to coat with the spices. Turn the heat off.

3. Rinse the spinach and place it in a large saucepan with a few tablespoons of water. Set the saucepan over medium heat and steam until the leaves wilt just a little, about 2 to 4 minutes. (Alternatively, you can steam the spinach in a vegetable steamer.) Drain the spinach in a colander to remove excess water, then divide it among 4 plates. Spoon some of the beet mixture over each bed of spinach and serve.

4 medium beets, peeled and
   cut in half
6 cups (1.5 L) water
2 Tbsp (30 mL) grapeseed oil
1 Tbsp (15 mL) dried
   fenugreek leaves
1 tsp (5 mL) fennel seeds
½ tsp (2 mL) ground cardamom
salt and pepper to taste
2 lb (1 kg) fresh spinach (about
   2 bunches)

Suggested wine

2006 Voluptuous by Van Westen Vineyards | This old world–style wine is a mix of Merlot and Cabernet Franc, with flavors of spice, chocolate, cherry, brown sugar, mineral, sagebrush, and coffee—a great combination with the fenugreek leaves, fennel seeds, and cardamom in this recipe.

56

I LOVE TO cook with tofu. One day I was looking for a quick finger food to make for my girlfriends and I came up with this recipe, which worked beautifully. *Serves 4*

1. **Heat the oil** in a skillet over medium-high heat. Once the oil is hot, add the tofu. Sear the tofu, turning until all sides are nicely golden brown. Reduce the heat to medium. Add the coriander, garam masala, paprika, salt, and lime juice, stirring to coat, and cook for 30 seconds longer.
2. Serve the tofu warm with cilantro chutney alongside.

2 Tbsp (30 mL) grapeseed oil
14 oz (430 g) package extra-firm
   tofu, cut into cubes
½ tsp (2 mL) ground coriander
½ tsp (2 mL) garam masala (page 7)
½ tsp (2 mL) Spanish paprika
salt to taste
1 Tbsp (15 mL) lime juice

CILANTRO CHUTNEY

Combine all the ingredients in a food processor or mortar and pestle, and process or pound until the cilantro is completely puréed. Refrigerate until ready to serve.

½ cup (125 mL) loosely
   packed cilantro
3 Tbsp (45 mL) water
1 Tbsp (15 mL) lime juice
1 small green chili, finely chopped
½ tsp (2 mL) ground cardamom

Soups

THE ONLY BEANS we ate in the village were kidney beans. Black beans were a new thing for me when I moved to Canada. I've enjoyed their nutty and earthy flavor ever since I tried them for the first time. *Serves 4*

Black beans should be on everyone's grocery list because they are inexpensive and versatile, contain fiber, and are a good source of both protein and iron.

2 Tbsp (30 mL) grapeseed oil

¼ cup (60 mL) finely chopped chives

1 Tbsp (15 mL) finely chopped garlic

1 Tbsp (15 mL) cumin seeds

1 Tbsp (15 mL) garam masala
   (page 7)

1 tsp (5 mL) ground turmeric

1 cup (250 mL) dried black beans,
   soaked overnight and rinsed

1 cup (250 mL) chopped tomatoes

¼ cup (60 mL) tamarind pulp
   (page 8)

7 cups (1.75 L) water

1. **Heat the oil** in a large saucepan over medium-high heat. When the oil is hot, add the chives, garlic, cumin seeds, garam masala, and turmeric and cook for 15 seconds. Stir in the black beans, tomatoes, and tamarind pulp and cook for 2 minutes.

2. Add the water and bring to a boil. Reduce the heat to low and cover the saucepan with a lid. Simmer until the beans are fully cooked, about 45 minutes to 1 hour.

AT THE HIGH school where I work as a teacher, we have a potluck lunch once a month, and everyone usually requests that I bring this soup, even though some of them have the recipe already. And every time, my colleagues comment on its aroma. I hope you enjoy the recipe—perhaps you can impress your colleagues, too.

Serves 4

Lentils are high in dietary fiber and protein and very low in fat.

Heat the oil in a large pot over medium-high heat. When the oil is hot, add the cumin seeds, garam masala, Ginger Masala, and curry leaves and cook for 10 seconds. Add the remaining ingredients and bring the mixture to a boil. Reduce the heat to low, cover, and simmer until the rice and lentils are cooked, 30 to 40 minutes.

2 Tbsp (30 mL) grapeseed oil
1 Tbsp (15 mL) cumin seeds
1 Tbsp (15 mL) garam masala (page 7)
1 tsp (5 mL) Ginger Masala (page 8)
6 to 8 curry leaves
6 cups (1.5 L) water
1 cup (250 mL) brown rice (uncooked)
1 cup (250 mL) split red lentils (*masoor dhal*)
1 cup (250 mL) chopped celery
1 cup (250 mL) coconut milk, fresh (sidebar page 100) or canned
¼ cup (60 mL) loosely packed cilantro, chopped
1 green chili, finely chopped
salt and pepper to taste

62

WHAT I LOVE here is the combination of textures, of the puréed cauliflower with whole chickpeas. I also love what the fenugreek and coriander add when sautéed with the chickpeas. I often prepare this for lunches.

Serves 4

1. **Combine the cauliflower**, water, salt, and pepper in a large saucepan. Bring to a boil, then cover, reduce the heat, and simmer until the cauliflower is tender, about 5 to 7 minutes. Let the mixture cool. Transfer the cauliflower and cooking liquid to a food processor and purée completely.

2. To prepare the chickpeas, heat the oil in a skillet over medium-high heat. When the oil is hot, add the garlic, coriander seeds, garam masala, fenugreek seeds, chili pepper flakes, and salt and cook for 15 seconds. Add the chickpeas and cook for 1 minute.

3. To serve, ladle 1 cup (250 mL) of the puréed cauliflower into each soup bowl and top with 2 Tbsp (30 mL) of the chickpea mixture. Garnish each serving with mint leaves, if desired.

Cauliflower

5 cups (1.25 L) chopped cauliflower

3 cups (750 mL) water

salt and pepper to taste

Chickpeas

1 Tbsp (15 mL) grapeseed oil

1 Tbsp (15 mL) finely chopped garlic

1 Tbsp (15 mL) coriander seeds, crushed

1 Tbsp (15 mL) garam masala (page 7)

1 tsp (5 mL) fenugreek seeds

½ tsp (2 mL) red chili pepper flakes

salt to taste

14 oz (398 mL) can chickpeas, drained and rinsed

fresh mint leaves for garnish (optional)

Suggested wine

2008 Pinot Gris by Poplar Grove

The rich, luscious, and mouth-filling pear, lemon, and tropical fruit flavors complement the fenugreek, coriander, and garam masala in the recipe.

SQUASH SOUP WITH
SOUTH INDIAN SPICES

IN THE VILLAGE, we often cooked with mustard seed oil but not often with actual mustard seeds. Curry leaves were also never used in my mother's kitchen. When I started experimenting as a cook, the magic blend of mustard seeds, curry leaves, and cumin inspired me to create several dishes, including this soup. I am a great fan of squash, and I especially love it in this recipe. Squash is delicious, versatile, and healthy, and I think it should be part of everyone's diet. *Serves 4*

Squash is an excellent source of vitamin A (in the form of beta-carotene) and a very good source of vitamin C, potassium, and fiber. It's also a good source of folate, omega-3 fatty acids, and B vitamins.

2 Tbsp (30 mL) grapeseed oil

1 Tbsp (15 mL) finely chopped garlic

1 Tbsp (15 mL) finely chopped ginger

1 Tbsp (15 mL) cumin seeds

1 Tbsp (15 mL) mustard seeds

1 Tbsp (15 mL) garam masala (page 7)

6 to 8 curry leaves

salt and pepper to taste

2 lb (1 kg) butternut or acorn squash, peeled and cut into small pieces

2 cups (500 mL) vegetable broth

1. **Heat the oil** in a skillet over medium-high heat. When the oil is hot, add the garlic and ginger and cook for 20 seconds. Add the cumin seeds, mustard seeds, garam masala, curry leaves, salt, and pepper and cook for 10 seconds.

2. Add the squash and vegetable broth and bring to a boil. Turn the heat to low, cover with a lid, and cook until the squash is fully tender, 7 to 9 minutes. Turn the heat off and allow the mixture to cool.

3. Transfer the mixture to a food processor and process until smooth. If it seems too thick, add a little water. Return the soup to the pot and reheat over medium heat before serving.

DHAL SOUP

ONE OF MY earliest tasks as a girl was to wash lentils for dhal soup, a staple in every Indian household. Picture me by the hand pump with a large pot of lentils! I took this task very seriously, using both my hands to pump the water, rubbing the lentils, draining them carefully, and making sure there was absolutely no dirt left and the water ran absolutely clear. Making this recipe always takes me back to the village and these lovely memories. *Serves 4*

Lentils, so rich in fiber, also provide several important minerals, B vitamins, and protein, and have virtually no fat.

2 Tbsp (30 mL) grapeseed oil

1 Tbsp (15 mL) finely chopped garlic

1 Tbsp (15 mL) cumin seeds

1 Tbsp (15 mL) garam masala (page 7)

1 tsp (5 mL) ground turmeric

salt and pepper to taste

1 cup (250 mL) finely chopped tomatoes

¼ cup (60 mL) finely chopped cilantro (more for garnish, if desired)

1 cup (250 mL) brown lentils

5 cups (1.25 L) water

1. **Heat the oil** in a skillet over medium-high heat. When the oil is hot, add the garlic, cumin seeds, garam masala, turmeric, salt, and pepper and cook for 20 seconds. Stir in the tomatoes and cilantro and cook for 2 minutes.

2. Add the lentils and water and bring to a boil. Turn the heat to low, cover with a lid, and cook until the lentils are soft and falling apart, about 30 to 40 minutes. Enjoy hot. Garnish with cilantro.

I ABSOLUTELY LOVE edamame. I've added fresh mint to this soup, but the secret spice here is the cardamom. And I've added fresh ginger at the end as a garnish and for additional flavor. Ginger has long been used as a natural treatment for colds and flu and has been used in folk medicine for thousands of years. So this soup is particularly beneficial during flu season but is healthy and delicious all year long. *Serves 4*

3 cups (750 mL) frozen
   shelled edamame
1 tsp (5 mL) fennel seeds
¼ tsp (1 mL) ground cardamom
salt and pepper to taste
1 cup (250 mL) water
¼ cup (60 mL) loosely packed
   mint leaves
1 tsp (5 mL) grapeseed oil
2-inch (5 cm) piece ginger, julienned

1. **Combine the edamame**, fennel seeds, cardamom, salt, pepper, and water in a saucepan and bring to a boil. Cover the saucepan, reduce the heat to low, and simmer for 3 to 5 minutes. Turn the heat off and allow the mixture to cool. Add the mint leaves.

2. Transfer the mixture to a blender and purée. Return the soup to the saucepan and reheat the soup gently on low heat.

3. Heat the oil in a small skillet over medium-high heat. When the oil is hot, add the ginger and fry for 15 seconds. Set it aside.

4. To serve, ladle the soup into 4 bowls. Garnish with a few pieces of the ginger in the center of each bowl.

GREEN PEA SOUP

EVERY TIME I visited my aunt in her distant village, she would make me green pea soup. I would help pick the fresh peas from her garden and collect the round green peas from each pod. To me the peas tasted like candy, so she would smack my hand each time I tried to eat them—she knew that, if it were up to me, I'd have eaten them all and there'd be nothing left for the soup!

Serves 4

Did you know that ***green peas*** are a very good source of folate and a good source of vitamin B6? They also contain good amounts of protein and fiber.

2 Tbsp (30 mL) grapeseed oil
1 Tbsp (15 mL) coriander seeds, crushed
1 tsp (5 mL) mustard seeds
1 tsp (5 mL) Turmeric Masala (page 8)
6 to 8 curry leaves
2 Tbsp (30 mL) tomato paste
⅛ tsp (0.5 mL) Spanish paprika
2 cups (500 mL) frozen peas
2 cups (500 mL) vegetable broth
½ cup (125 mL) plain yogurt

1. ***Heat the oil*** in a skillet over medium-high heat. When the oil is hot, add the coriander seeds, mustard seeds, Turmeric Masala, and curry leaves. Reduce the heat to medium and cook for 10 seconds. Add the tomato paste and paprika and cook for 20 seconds. Stir in the peas, broth, and yogurt and bring to a boil. Cover the skillet, reduce the heat to low, and cook for 5 minutes.

2. Remove the skillet from the heat and allow the mixture to cool. Transfer the mixture to a food processor and process until smooth.

3. Serve this soup either warm or cold.

SQUASH AND PAPAYA SOUP

ONE OF THE reasons I love fall is seeing all the beautiful, colorful squashes at the farmers' markets. This dish blends the sweet flavors of squash and papaya with beautifully colored spices to make a perfect autumn dish.
Serves 4

Squash is a very good source of vitamin C, potassium, and fiber, and **papayas** are rich in antioxidants and B vitamins. This soup is like a delicious tonic!

1. **Heat the oil** in a skillet over medium-high heat. When the oil is hot, add the garam masala, mustard seeds, fennel seeds, and fenugreek leaves and cook for 10 seconds. Stir in the squash, turmeric, salt, pepper, and water and bring to a boil. Cover the skillet, then reduce the heat to medium-low and simmer until the squash is tender, about 7 minutes. Remove from the heat and allow the mixture to cool.
2. Add the papaya pulp to the skillet, then transfer the mixture to a blender and purée until smooth.
3. Serve warm.

2 Tbsp (30 mL) grapeseed oil
1 Tbsp (15 mL) garam masala (page 7)
1 tsp (5 mL) mustard seeds
1 tsp (5 mL) fennel seeds
1 tsp (5 mL) dried fenugreek leaves
1 lb (500 g) winter squash (e.g., butternut or acorn), peeled and cut into bite-sized pieces
½ tsp (2 mL) ground turmeric
salt and pepper to taste
4 cups (1 L) water
1 medium-sized ripe papaya, seeds removed, flesh scooped out and mashed with a fork

72

MY FIRST TASTE of tomato soup was when I first visited my uncle in the huge city of Delhi. It was a bowl of extremely rich and creamy tomato soup. I realized that city people used cream in their cooking much more regularly than in the village, where cream was used only on special occasions, like feasts or weddings. This is a much healthier version than the one I tried long ago in Delhi—no cream! *Serves 4*

Tomatoes are an excellent source of vitamin C and vitamin A and are also very high in fiber.

1. **Heat the oil** in a saucepan over medium-high heat. When the oil is hot, add the garlic, garam masala, Turmeric Masala, salt, and pepper and cook for 20 seconds. Stir in the crushed tomatoes and vegetable broth and bring to a boil. Turn the heat to low, cover, and cook for about 8 to 10 minutes.
2. Add the fennel seeds to the soup, then remove it from the heat. Serve hot.

2 Tbsp (30 mL) grapeseed oil

1 Tbsp (15 mL) finely chopped garlic

1 tsp (5 mL) garam masala (page 7)

1 tsp (5 mL) Turmeric Masala (page 8)

salt and pepper to taste

28 oz (796 mL) can crushed tomatoes

1½ cups (375 mL) vegetable broth

1 Tbsp (15 mL) fennel seeds

Suggested wine

2008 rosé by Monster Vineyards

This mixture of Merlot and Syrah, with its flavors of strawberry cordial and mint tea, works beautifully with the garlic and fennel in the soup.

Meat

MEATBALLS WITH PANEER AND CASHEWS

NUTS SUCH AS cashews and almonds were rare when I was growing up—much rarer than peanuts. When we had them, I would sometimes sneak into our pantry for a taste. I really appreciate now the luxury of using these nuts. These meatballs are a great addition to pasta.
Serves 4

Cashews are high in monounsaturated fats and are a good source of copper and magnesium.

1. **Soak the cashews** in warm water for 20 minutes, then drain them, reserving 2 Tbsp (30 mL) of the soaking water. Place the cashews and reserved water in a food processor and process to a paste, or crush by hand in a mortar and pestle.

2. Combine the ground cashews with the remaining ingredients, except the oil, in a bowl and mix well. Form the mixture into meatballs about the size of golf balls.

3. Heat the oil in a nonstick pan over medium-high heat. When the oil is hot, reduce the heat to medium and carefully place the meatballs in the pan, making sure they do not touch each other. Fry the meatballs until they are fully cooked, about 8 to 10 minutes, turning them frequently so that all sides are browned. (To ensure the meatballs are cooked through, break one open slightly to make sure there is no pink inside.)

4. Serve on the side with Dhal Soup (page 66).

¼ cup (60 mL) cashews
½ lb (250 g) ground beef
½ lb (250 g) paneer (page 10), crumbled
1 Tbsp (15 mL) finely chopped ginger
1 Tbsp (15 mL) ground cumin
1 Tbsp (15 mL) coriander seeds, crushed
1 tsp (5 mL) Turmeric Masala (page 8)
salt to taste
¼ cup (60 mL) grapeseed oil

I COOK WITH fresh as well as dried figs. There's a more intense sweetness to dried figs, and this sweetness combines with aromatic spices to perfectly complement beef. *Serves 4*

Because **figs** are high in fiber and contain calcium and iron, we have even more reason to enjoy this dish.

1. **Heat the oil** in a skillet over medium-high heat. When the oil is hot, add the ginger and cook for 20 seconds. Add the Ginger Masala, cardamom, turmeric, and salt and cook for 10 more seconds.

2. Add the sirloin and stir-fry for about 3 minutes. Add the figs and continue to stir-fry for about 2 more minutes, until the sirloin is cooked through.

3. Meanwhile, rinse the spinach and place it in a vegetable steamer, or place it in a large saucepan with a few tablespoons of water and set it over medium heat. Steam the spinach until the leaves wilt just a little, about 2 to 4 minutes. Drain the spinach in a colander to remove excess water and divide it among 4 plates over rice, if serving. Top with the sirloin. Enjoy!

1 Tbsp (15 mL) grapeseed oil

1 Tbsp (15 mL) finely chopped ginger

1 Tbsp (15 mL) Ginger Masala (page 8)

1 tsp (5 mL) ground cardamom

½ tsp (2 mL) ground turmeric

½ tsp (2 mL) salt

2 lb (1 kg) sirloin steak, thinly sliced

½ cup (125 mL) chopped dried figs

4 cups (1 L) loosely packed fresh spinach, chopped

Suggested wine
2005 Sette Coppa by D'Angelo

I love this wine, a blend of the classic varieties Merlot, Cabernet Franc, Cabernet Sauvignon, Petit Verdot, and Malbec. Its flavors of ripe plum, cherry, and strawberry are an excellent complement to the cardamom and figs.

SPICES CAN CREATE a wonderful, tasty crust for sirloin. The fenugreek—in the form of both leaves and ground seeds—is especially aromatic. This is a delicious way to transform a typical meat-and-potatoes dinner into something special. *Serves 4*

Fenugreek seeds contain vitamin C, niacin, and potassium. I was so excited to learn this that I called my friend in the village. She responded: "Of course! All spices are healthy." Indeed, there is more and more scientific research proving the amazing benefits of spices—something village women have known for countless generations.

1. **Preheat the barbecue** to medium-high heat. (If using wooden skewers, soak them in water for 30 minutes before using.)

2. To prepare the sirloin, combine all the seasonings in a large bowl. Add the sirloin pieces and stir until they are well coated with the spice mixture. Thread the meat onto skewers.

3. Place the skewers on the preheated barbecue and grill until the meat is cooked to the desired level of doneness—about 4 minutes for medium-rare, or about 6 minutes for well done. Keep turning the skewers while grilling to make sure all sides are cooked well.

Sirloin

¼ cup (60 mL) dried
    fenugreek leaves
1 Tbsp (15 mL) garam masala
    (page 7)
1 tsp (5 mL) Ginger Masala (page 8)
1 tsp (5 mL) ground cumin
¼ tsp (1 mL) ground turmeric
⅛ tsp (0.5 mL) ground fenugreek
    (seeds)
salt and pepper to taste
1 lb (500 g) sirloin steak, cut into
    1-inch (2.5 cm) pieces
6 metal or wooden skewers

Roasted potatoes

1 lb (500 g) small red potatoes,
    halved
2 Tbsp (30 mL) grapeseed oil
1 Tbsp (15 mL) finely
    chopped ginger
1 tsp (5 mL) coriander seeds,
    crushed
salt and pepper to taste

4. Meanwhile, place the potatoes in a saucepan with enough water to cover and bring to a boil. Cover the saucepan and turn the heat to medium. Cook until the potatoes are almost tender, about 8 to 10 minutes. Drain the water.

5. Heat the oil in a skillet over medium-high heat. When the oil is hot, add the ginger and cook for 15 seconds. Add the coriander seeds, salt, and pepper and cook for 10 more seconds. Add the partially cooked potatoes to the pan, stirring to coat them well with the oil and spices. Continue cooking, stirring regularly, until the potatoes are tender, 2 to 4 minutes.

6. Serve the sirloin skewers and potatoes with Cherry Tomato and Cucumber Salad with Capers and Fig Dressing (page 28).

SIRLOIN STIR-FRY WITH FRESH TOMATOES AND BROCCOLI

I OFTEN MAKE stir-fries as they make a quick and very nutritious meal for my hungry family. You can easily adapt this recipe depending on what you have on hand and use any of your favorite vegetables or meats. Not that I usually have any leftovers for the next day, but if I do, they are great for lunches. *Serves 4*

I love **broccoli** as it is a great source of fiber, calcium, and vitamin C.

2 Tbsp (30 mL) grapeseed oil
1 Tbsp (15 mL) finely chopped garlic
1 Tbsp (15 mL) ground cumin
1 tsp (5 mL) mustard seeds
salt and pepper to taste
1 lb (500 g) sirloin steak,
   thinly sliced
1 cup (250 mL) chopped tomatoes
1 lb (500 g) broccoli, separated
   into florets

1. **Heat the oil** in a wok over medium-high heat. When the oil is hot, add the garlic, cumin, mustard seeds, salt, and pepper and cook for 20 seconds. Add the sirloin and stir-fry until it is almost cooked, about 3 to 4 minutes.
2. Add the tomatoes and broccoli and continue sautéing until the sirloin is cooked through, about 2 minutes.
3. Serve over rice, accompanied by Black Bean Soup with Cumin and Garlic (page 60).

SPICED LAMB
WITH COCONUT SAUCE

YOU CAN ADD a totally new flavor to lamb just by using spices and fresh coconut. Friends have told me that after eating this they can never enjoy lamb cooked any other way! Fresh coconut is the special ingredient here. The flavor and texture may be a luxury, but you should really look for it to make this recipe. *Serves 4*

Coconut is highly nutritious and full of fiber, and provides several vitamins and minerals—another reason to enjoy this delicious dish.

1. **Heat the oil** in a skillet over medium-high heat. When the oil is hot, add the garlic and cook for 10 seconds, stirring. Add the cumin seeds, coriander seeds, cardamom, fennel seeds, Turmeric Masala, curry leaves, salt, and pepper and cook for 20 seconds. Stir in the lamb and cook for 3 to 5 minutes. Add the coconut and cook for 2 minutes, stirring regularly.
2. Stir in the tomatoes, onions, and vegetable broth, then reduce the heat to low. Simmer until the lamb is cooked through and tender, about 20 to 25 minutes.
3. Serve with rice and Avocado and Chickpea Salad (page 14).

2 Tbsp (30 mL) grapeseed oil
1 Tbsp (15 mL) finely chopped garlic
1 Tbsp (15 mL) cumin seeds
1 Tbsp (15 mL) coriander seeds, crushed
1 tsp (5 mL) ground cardamom
1 tsp (5 mL) fennel seeds
½ tsp (2 mL) Turmeric Masala (page 8)
8 to 10 curry leaves
salt and pepper to taste
1 lb (500 g) stewing lamb, cut into pieces
1 cup (250 mL) grated fresh coconut (sidebar page 100) or unsweetened dried coconut flakes
1 cup (250 mL) finely chopped tomatoes
2 large onions, thinly sliced
2 cups (500 mL) vegetable broth

84

IF IT WERE up to me, I would add mangoes to everything. In this dish, garam masala balances the sweetness of the mango. I had originally planned to use raw sugar, but with mangoes in season, I used them instead. The result is absolutely delicious. In this recipe, I am also using mango juice, which can be purchased in a box or a bottle from most grocery stores. *Serves 4*

Mangoes are a rich source of vitamin A and antioxidants. If only I had known all this when I was a child. Whenever I'd climb up the mango tree, my mother would frown and tell me only boys were allowed to do the climbing. I would have responded by listing the health properties of mangoes to justify my mango picking!

1. **Heat the oil** in a deep skillet over medium-high heat. When the oil is hot, add the onion, garlic, and ginger and cook, stirring regularly, until the onion starts to soften and turn brown, about 4 minutes. Add the garam masala, cumin seeds, coriander seeds, turmeric, and salt and cook for 30 seconds. Add the tomato paste and cook for another 30 seconds. Add the lamb, then brown for 3 to 5 minutes, stirring occasionally.

2. Stir in the crushed tomatoes, mango juice, vegetable broth, and green chilies and bring the mixture to a boil. Turn the heat to low, cover the skillet, and simmer, stirring regularly, until the lamb is soft, 45 minutes to 1 hour.

3. Add the mango pieces to the skillet, turn the heat off, cover, and let it sit for 10 minutes before serving.

4. Serve with rice and White Radish Salad with Cherry Dressing (page 29).

3 Tbsp (45 mL) grapeseed oil

1 medium onion, finely chopped

1 Tbsp (15 mL) finely chopped garlic

1 Tbsp (15 mL) finely
    chopped ginger

1 Tbsp (15 mL) garam masala
    (page 7)

1 Tbsp (15 mL) cumin seeds

1 Tbsp (15 mL) coriander seeds,
    crushed

1 tsp (5 mL) ground turmeric

salt to taste

2 Tbsp (30 mL) tomato paste

1 lb (500 g) stewing lamb,
    cut into pieces

14 oz (398 mL) can crushed tomatoes

1 cup (250 mL) mango juice

1 cup (250 mL) vegetable broth

2 medium green chilies,
    finely chopped

1 large ripe mango, peeled, pitted,
    and cut into bite-sized pieces

Suggested wine

2008 Pink Elephant by Elephant Island Orchard Wines | I love how the currant and green apple aromatics of this wine play off the flavors of the cumin, coriander, and mango juice. A great wine choice and a great pairing!

86

I DO NOT cook this very often—it's more of a treat for me. I get out my fine dishes when I serve this dish, especially if I am celebrating with my girlfriends over. The whole day ends up being a special occasion, from going to the local butcher to pouring myself a glass of wine while I cook.

Ripe pears make a fabulous chutney. It's a wonderful accompaniment to the spices used for the pork.

Serves 4

Pears are rich in copper, phosphorus, and potassium and are an excellent source of soluble fiber. They also contain vitamins A, B1, B2, C, E, folate, and niacin.

2 Tbsp (30 mL) grapeseed oil

1 Tbsp (15 mL) coriander seeds, crushed

1 Tbsp (15 mL) garam masala (page 7)

1 tsp (5 mL) ground cardamom

1 tsp (5 mL) mustard seeds

1 tsp (5 mL) ground turmeric

6 to 8 curry leaves

2 lb (1 kg) pork rib roast (4 ribs)

1 cup (250 mL) unsweetened dried coconut flakes

1 cup (250 mL) coconut milk

salt and pepper to taste

1. **Preheat the oven** to 425°F (220°C).
2. Heat the oil in an ovenproof skillet over medium-high heat. Add the coriander seeds, garam masala, cardamom, mustard seeds, turmeric, and curry leaves and cook for 10 seconds. Add the pork, flesh side down, and sear until golden brown, 4 to 6 minutes. Stir in the coconut flakes, coconut milk, salt, and pepper and cook for 2 more minutes.
3. Place the skillet in the preheated oven and roast for 30 minutes. Remove from the oven. Transfer the meat to a cutting board and tent with foil for 10 to 15 minutes before slicing.
4. Serve with pear chutney accompanied by Sugar Snap Peas with Maple Syrup and Coriander (page 118).

PEAR CHUTNEY

Place all the chutney ingredients in a food processor and process until smooth. Refrigerate until ready to serve.

2 extra-ripe pears, peeled, cored, and cubed
¼ cup (60 mL) chopped red onion
¼ cup (60 mL) water
1 Tbsp (15 mL) lemon juice
½ tsp (2 mL) garam masala (page 7)
salt and pepper to taste

WHEN I CREATED this recipe, I immediately called to tell my lovely friend Cheryl, who originally introduced me to pork tenderloin. She wondered about using other herbs and spices and I said, go ahead! Most of my recipes are based on whatever I have in my fridge, garden, and pantry, I told her. You should try cooking this way, too, trusting your palate as a guide. Cheryl used basil, thyme, and garam masala with great success. Don't forget to be spontaneous and have fun in the kitchen.

I always try to use fresh coconut in a recipe, but it is often not the season for it. I use unsweetened dried coconut and it works just fine. I have used frozen coconut as well; when thawed, it is almost like fresh. *Serves 4*

1 cup (250 mL) grated fresh coconut (sidebar page 100)

¼ cup (60 mL) water

2 Tbsp (30 mL) liquid honey

2 Tbsp (30 mL) finely chopped mint

2 Tbsp (30 mL) finely chopped cilantro

1 Tbsp (15 mL) ground cumin

1 Tbsp (15 mL) ground coriander

1 tsp (5 mL) Spanish paprika

salt to taste

2 pork tenderloins, about 13 oz (400 g) each

1. **Preheat the barbecue** to medium-high heat.
2. In a medium bowl, combine the coconut, water, honey, mint, cilantro, cumin, coriander, paprika, and salt. Rub the mixture onto all sides of the tenderloins. Set aside any remaining coconut sauce.
3. Grill the tenderloins, turning them every 10 minutes and brushing them with the reserved coconut sauce. Cook until the internal temperature reaches 160°F (71°C), about 30 to 40 minutes. Remove the pork from the grill and let it sit for 5 to 10 minutes before slicing.
4. Serve with Grilled Mushrooms, Asparagus, and Red Pepper with Tofu (page 145).

CHICKEN BREASTS STUFFED WITH PANEER, BLACK BEANS, AND TOMATOES

PANEER WAS MADE only on special occasions in the village, but I always longed for it. Now I can have it all the time, and I do, since it is so easy and quick to make and my family just loves it. Of course, they don't realize how privileged they are! Paneer fills these chicken breasts with rich flavors and transforms them into an exotic dish that everyone adores. *Serves 4*

Black beans are very high in dietary fiber, and provide a good source of protein, iron, and antioxidants. Use them generously!

1. **Preheat the oven** to 375°F (190°C).
2. Heat the oil in a skillet over medium-high heat. When the oil is hot, add the ginger, fennel seeds, coriander seeds, fenugreek leaves, 1 Tbsp (15 mL) of the garam masala, salt, and pepper and cook for 30 seconds. Add the black beans, cherry tomatoes, tomato sauce, and paneer and cook for 3 to 5 minutes, stirring frequently.
3. Divide the paneer mixture in two. To stuff the breasts, cut them partway. Fill the chicken breasts with one-half of the paneer mixture.
4. In a 2-inch-deep (5 cm) baking pan, place the rest of the paneer mixture along with the tomatoes, vegetable broth, the remaining 1 Tbsp (15 mL) garam masala, and salt. Stir with a spoon. Gently place the stuffed chicken breasts on top of the paneer mixture.
5. Cover the baking pan with foil and place it in the middle rack of the oven. Bake for 40 to 50 minutes, until the chicken is cooked through.
6. Serve with rice and Mixed Vegetables with Fennel and Cumin Seeds (page 144).

2 Tbsp (30 mL) grapeseed oil
1 Tbsp (15 mL) finely chopped ginger
1 Tbsp (15 mL) fennel seeds
1 Tbsp (15 mL) coriander seeds, crushed
1 Tbsp (15 mL) dried fenugreek leaves
2 Tbsp (30 mL) garam masala (page 7) (divided)
salt and pepper to taste
2 cups (500 mL) cooked black beans (if using canned, drain and rinse before using)
1 cup (250 mL) halved cherry tomatoes
1 cup (250 mL) canned tomato sauce
½ lb (250 g) paneer (page 10), crumbled
4 boneless, skinless chicken breasts
4 cups (1 L) chopped tomatoes
1 cup (250 mL) vegetable broth
¼ tsp (1 mL) salt

GRILLED CHICKEN
WITH CORIANDER

CORIANDER SEED HAS a very warm and nutty taste. I use both crushed and ground coriander here. I suggest using chicken with the skin on as the skin adds flavor and keeps the chicken juicy. Serve with brown basmati rice, or over a simple green salad with a light lemon dressing. *Serves 4*

Coriander seeds are a good source of iron and magnesium. This is a yummy, easy-to-prepare, and heart-healthy dish!

2 Tbsp (30 mL) grapeseed oil
1 Tbsp (15 mL) finely chopped garlic
2 Tbsp (30 mL) coriander seeds, crushed
1 Tbsp (15 mL) ground coriander
½ tsp (2 mL) ground cardamom
salt and pepper to taste
4 boneless chicken breasts, skin on

1. **Combine the oil**, garlic, coriander seeds, ground coriander, cardamom, salt, and pepper in a shallow bowl and mix well. Prick the chicken all over with a fork, then rub the spice mixture on both sides of each chicken breast. Set aside any remaining spice mixture. Place the chicken in a dish, cover, and refrigerate for at least 30 minutes or up to 6 hours.
2. Preheat the barbecue to medium heat.
3. Place the chicken skin side down on the grill. Brush with the remaining spice mixture and grill until the chicken is cooked through, about 30 to 40 minutes. Check the inside of the chicken: there should be no pink showing. Slice the chicken pieces on the diagonal.
4. Serve with rice and Okra with Egg Noodles (page 142).

GRILLED CHICKEN IN YOGURT

MY FAVORITE PART of the chicken is the thighs; this dark meat is tender and very flavorful. Sometimes instead of grilling I cook this chicken in the oven in a covered pot and add lots of fresh tomatoes and chicken broth. You should try it this way, too: I promise you will love it either way. *Serves 4*

You can serve this with rice or rotis, but I like to serve it with ***asparagus***, which is an excellent source of folate, vitamin C, vitamin A, and potassium and provides fiber and protein.

1 cup (250 mL) plain yogurt
1 Tbsp (15 mL) garam masala (page 7)
1 tsp (5 mL) ground fennel
1 tsp (5 mL) ground coriander
1 tsp (5 mL) finely chopped garlic
1 tsp (5 mL) freshly grated ginger
1 tsp (5 mL) Spanish paprika
1 tsp (5 mL) salt
1 lb (500 g) chicken thighs, bone in and skin on

1. **In a large bowl**, combine the yogurt, garam masala, fennel, coriander, garlic, ginger, paprika, and salt. Mix well. Add the chicken thighs to the mixture and marinate in the fridge for at least 30 minutes or up to 4 hours.
2. Preheat the barbecue to medium-high heat.
3. Place the chicken on the rack and grill, turning regularly to ensure both sides are cooked equally, until cooked through, about 30 to 40 minutes.
4. Serve over brown rice or steamed asparagus. (To steam asparagus, snap off the ends and place the stalks in a steamer for 3 to 5 minutes.)

AS WITH OTHER green veggies, bok choy is very nutritious. Bok choy's unique flavor is particularly enticing when the vegetable is steamed. I was surprised how perfectly Indian spices go with this Chinese vegetable.

Serves 4

Bok choy contains powerful antioxidants. It is also high in vitamin C, beta-carotene, calcium, and fiber. Sometimes I use it instead of spinach in cooked dishes.

2 Tbsp (30 mL) grapeseed oil

2 Tbsp (30 mL) finely chopped garlic

2 Tbsp (30 mL) finely chopped ginger

salt and pepper to taste

2 boneless, skinless chicken breasts, each halved lengthwise

1 Tbsp (15 mL) ground fennel

1 tsp (5 mL) ground cardamom

1 lb (500 g) bok choy, chopped

1. **Preheat the barbecue** to medium-high heat.
2. In a small bowl, combine the oil, garlic, ginger, salt, and pepper. Place the chicken breasts on a plate and brush the oil mixture on all sides.
3. Turn the barbecue down to medium and gently place the chicken on the grill. Cook, turning frequently, until the chicken is cooked through and all sides are nicely browned, about 20 minutes. Remove the chicken from the barbecue and sprinkle it with the fennel and cardamom.
4. Steam the bok choy in a vegetable steamer for 3 to 5 minutes.
5. If you don't have a steamer, place a colander in a saucepan. Fill the saucepan with water, making sure the water does not touch the colander. Place the bok choy in the colander and cover the saucepan with a lid or foil. Bring the water to boil, then reduce the heat to medium-low and steam for 3 to 5 minutes.
6. While the bok choy is cooking, prepare the Strawberry and Kiwi Salad (page 94).

Suggested wine

2007 Merlot/Cabernet Sauvignon by Township 7 | A balanced and bold wine with rich, textured flavors of raspberry and blackberry, which pair nicely with the smoky flavor of the barbecue and garam masala in this dish.

continued

7. To serve, place some steamed bok choy on each plate, gently place a piece of chicken on top, and top with a scoop of the Strawberry and Kiwi Salad.

STRAWBERRY AND KIWI SALAD

Serves 4

In a medium bowl, combine all the ingredients and stir them together well.

1 cup (250 mL) finely chopped strawberries
½ cup (125 mL) finely chopped kiwi
1 Tbsp (15 mL) lemon juice
⅛ tsp (0.5 mL) garam masala (page 7)
salt and pepper to taste

CHICKEN MASALA WITH CHERRY TOMATOES AND SPINACH

THE ONLY TIME spinach was cooked in my mother's kitchen was for *saag*, a vegetarian dish with spinach, rapini, and corn flour, so it never occurred to me to combine spinach with meat. But of course spinach goes wonderfully with chicken! Especially if the spinach is barely cooked and the whole thing is served in a flavorful garam masala sauce. *Serves 4*

Spinach is rich in vitamin A and fiber and contains nutrients such as calcium, folate, vitamin K, and iron. The beautiful dark green leaves are so healthy and delicious that I was surprised to learn that here in North America spinach is sometimes not appreciated. I love spinach, so I am on a mission to change that!

2 Tbsp (30 mL) grapeseed oil
1 Tbsp (15 mL) finely chopped garlic
1 Tbsp (15 mL) cumin seeds
1 Tbsp (15 mL) coriander seeds, crushed
1 Tbsp (15 mL) garam masala (page 7)
1 tsp (5 mL) ground turmeric
salt to taste
1 lb (500 g) boneless, skinless chicken breasts, cut into bite-sized pieces
2 cups (500 mL) whole cherry tomatoes
1 lb (500 g) fresh spinach, chopped

1. **Heat the oil** in a skillet over medium-high heat. When the oil is hot, add the garlic, cumin seeds, coriander seeds, and garam masala and cook for 10 seconds. Add the turmeric, salt, and chicken and sauté for about 6 minutes, until the chicken is partially cooked.
2. Stir in the cherry tomatoes and spinach and continue sautéing until the chicken is cooked through, another 6 to 8 minutes.
3. Serve over rice with Tamarind Mushrooms (page 138) on the side.

96

ALMOND BUTTER NOT only gives this recipe a beautiful flavor but also makes the sauce creamy. The almond butter goes so well with the spices that it seems like a beautifully arranged marriage—no kidding! I use this ingredient regularly now. *Serves 4*

Almonds are a good source of monounsaturated fats, vitamin E, magnesium, and potassium.

2 Tbsp (30 mL) grapeseed oil
2 Tbsp (30 mL) finely chopped garlic
1 Tbsp (15 mL) fenugreek seeds
1 Tbsp (15 mL) cumin seeds
1 Tbsp (15 mL) ground coriander
salt and pepper to taste
2 lb (1 kg) boneless, skinless chicken
    breasts, cut into bite-sized pieces
1 cup (250 mL) chopped tomatoes
1 cup (250 mL) chopped red pepper
¼ cup (60 mL) almond butter

1. **Heat the oil** in a skillet over medium-high heat. When the oil is hot, add the garlic, fenugreek seeds, cumin seeds, coriander, salt, and pepper and cook for 5 seconds. Add the chicken and cook for 5 minutes, stirring regularly.
2. Stir in the tomatoes, red pepper, and almond butter. Turn the heat to low and cover the skillet with a lid. Simmer until the chicken is cooked through, another 3 to 5 minutes.
3. Serve over rice with Shiitake Mushrooms with Fennel Seeds (page 141) on the side.

FENUGREEK CHICKEN

I WAS LESS than five years old, helping my mother in the herb garden, when I was first introduced to fresh fenugreek. I can still remember how beautiful it smelled. In this recipe, I use fenugreek in two of its culinary manifestations: as dried leaves and ground fenugreek seeds.

Serves 4

½ cup (125 mL) all-purpose flour

1 Tbsp (15 mL) dried fenugreek leaves

1 Tbsp (15 mL) garam masala (page 7)

1 tsp (5 mL) Ginger Masala (page 8)

1 tsp (5 mL) salt

½ tsp (2 mL) ground fenugreek (seeds)

¼ tsp (1 mL) pepper

2 eggs

4 boneless, skinless chicken breasts, each halved lengthwise

2 Tbsp (30 mL) grapeseed oil

1. **Preheat the oven** to 350°F (175°C).

2. Combine the flour, fenugreek leaves, garam masala, Ginger Masala, salt, ground fenugreek, and pepper in a shallow bowl or a pie plate. In a separate shallow bowl, beat the eggs. Dip each chicken piece in the egg, then coat in the flour mixture.

3. Heat the oil in a nonstick skillet over medium-high heat. When the oil is hot, carefully place the chicken pieces in the pan. When they are browned on the bottom, flip and brown the other sides.

4. Transfer the chicken to a nonstick baking sheet and bake until cooked through, about 25 to 35 minutes.

5. Serve with Indian-Style Red Potatoes and Mixed Vegetables (page 116).

98

MY 17-YEAR-OLD DAUGHTER, Anoop, goes through mood swings when it comes to food. She was a vegetarian one month, and the next it was only seafood that she loved. And when she didn't want to eat any red meat, that's when I came up with this chicken burger recipe. Many times when Anoop's friends call and I pick up the phone, they invite themselves over with a request that I make these! If teenagers like a recipe, you know it's a good one to add to your cookbook. I think the secret here is the tangy tamarind and the spicy masalas.

Serves 4

Tamarind is a good source of antioxidants, vitamin C, and B vitamins.

1 lb (500 g) ground chicken

½ cup (125 mL) unsweetened dried coconut flakes

¼ cup (60 mL) tamarind pulp (page 8)

1 Tbsp (15 mL) finely chopped garlic

1 Tbsp (15 mL) garam masala (page 7)

1 Tbsp (15 mL) Tandoori Masala (page 8)

salt and pepper to taste

1. **Preheat a barbecue** or grill to medium heat.
2. Combine all the ingredients in a bowl, stirring with a large spoon until well blended. Form into burger patties.
3. Place the burger patties on the preheated barbecue. Grill the burgers for 8 to 10 minutes, flipping them after 2 to 3 minutes.
4. Serve as a burger on a bun or in a pita, accompanied with Banana Squash with Green Chilies and Fenugreek Seeds (page 131), or serve the patty on its own with rice and vegetables.

100

EVERY WOMAN IN the village had her own way of making coconut milk. The method I use now is simple and easy (see the sidebar). The first time I made my own, it was so delicious that I drank all of it myself. I shared my next batch with a few of my girlfriends, but this time we added a little rum to it. It was even more delicious! We did have a little bit left over so I decided to cook with it, and this is the result. When I don't have fresh coconut, I substitute canned coconut milk, which is much creamier. *Serves 4*

1. **Heat the oil** in a skillet over medium-high heat. When the oil is hot, add the ginger and cook for 10 seconds. While stirring, add the coriander seeds, garam masala, and cardamom and cook for 10 seconds. Stir in the tomato paste and cook for another 10 seconds. Add the coconut flakes, salt, and pepper and cook for 1 minute.

2. Add the chicken to the mixture, lower the heat to medium, and cook for 5 to 7 minutes, stirring regularly. Stir in the coconut milk, reduce the heat to low, and cook for another 5 minutes.

3. Serve over brown rice with Green Beans and Paneer in Fresh Tomato Sauce (page 111).

2 Tbsp (30 mL) grapeseed oil

1 Tbsp (15 mL) finely chopped ginger

2 Tbsp (30 mL) coriander seeds, crushed

1 Tbsp (15 mL) garam masala (page 7)

1 tsp (5 mL) ground cardamom

2 Tbsp (30 mL) tomato paste

½ cup (125 mL) unsweetened dried coconut flakes

salt and pepper to taste

2 lb (1 kg) boneless, skinless chicken breasts, cut into bite-sized pieces

½ cup (125 mL) fresh coconut milk (see sidebar)

Fresh coconut

Pierce the shell of a coconut with a nail and break it open. Drain the coconut water into a large bowl. Remove the coconut meat from the hard outer husk. (There's a thin brown skin on the meat, which I do not remove.) For fresh coconut milk, place the coconut water and the coconut meat in a blender and process until smooth.

CHICKEN THIGHS WITH TOMATOES AND EGGPLANT

WE GREW EGGPLANT in our vegetable garden, and it was amazing to see how much one plant could produce. I would put the abundance of eggplants in a large basket to carry on my head as I went from home to home, giving them away. We used eggplant for only two dishes: *bartha*, which involved baking and peeling the eggplant and then cooking the pulp with onions; and *btaun*, which involved cutting the eggplant into large pieces and cooking them with potatoes, tomatoes, ginger, and onions. This was one of my first eggplant recipes with meat, and I am very pleased with the results. *Serves 4*

Eggplant contains dietary fiber, vitamins B1 and B6, and potassium.

2 Tbsp (30 mL) grapeseed oil

1 Tbsp (15 mL) finely chopped ginger

1 Tbsp (15 mL) finely chopped garlic

2 Tbsp (30 mL) dried fenugreek leaves

1 Tbsp (15 mL) ground coriander

1 tsp (5 mL) mustard seeds

2 lb (1 kg) chicken thighs, bone in and skin on

1 lb (500 g) eggplant, finely chopped

½ cup (125 mL) loosely packed cilantro, chopped

salt and pepper to taste

2 cups (500 mL) chicken broth

1 cup (250 mL) chopped tomatoes

½ cup (125 mL) plain yogurt

1. **Heat the oil** in a skillet over medium-high heat. When the oil is hot, add the ginger and garlic and cook for 20 seconds. Add the fenugreek leaves, coriander, and mustard seeds and cook for 10 seconds. Add the chicken, eggplant, cilantro, salt, and pepper and cook for 5 minutes, stirring regularly.

2. Stir in the chicken broth, tomatoes, and yogurt. Reduce the heat to low, cover the skillet, and simmer until the chicken is fully cooked, 10 to 15 minutes.

3. Serve with rice and Spiced Sweet Potatoes Cooked with Split Red Lentils (page 124).

ON SPECIAL OCCASIONS, my aunts and my mother cooked a recipe similar to this, in a large copper pot that was placed over a barbecue pit of newly dug clay. The sauce would have heaping tablespoons of green chilies, garlic, ginger, and garam masala. I've added spinach as it gives the sauce an almost creamy consistency that is perfect with the chicken. *Serves 4*

Spinach is rich in vitamin A and fiber and is also a source of calcium and iron.

1. **To prepare the spinach sauce**, heat the oil in a skillet over medium-high heat. When the oil is hot, add the cumin seeds and cardamom and cook for 10 seconds. Add the spinach, tomatoes, green chili, garlic, salt, and water and reduce the heat to low. Cook until the spinach is wilted, about 3 to 4 minutes.
2. Remove from the heat and allow the mixture to cool. Transfer to a blender or a food processor and process until smooth. Set aside.
3. To prepare the chicken, heat the oil in a skillet over medium-high heat. When the oil is hot, add the garam masala and ginger and cook for 15 seconds. Add the chicken, lower the heat to medium, and cook, stirring regularly, for 9 to 12 minutes, until the chicken is cooked through.
4. Add the spinach sauce to the chicken and cook for 2 minutes longer, then remove from the heat.
5. Serve over rice, accompanied by Fenugreek Cabbage with Chickpeas (page 134).

Spinach sauce
2 Tbsp (30 mL) grapeseed oil
1 Tbsp (15 mL) cumin seeds
1 tsp (5 mL) ground cardamom
2 lb (1 kg) fresh spinach, chopped
1 cup (250 mL) finely
    chopped tomatoes
1 small green chili, finely chopped
1 Tbsp (15 mL) finely chopped garlic
salt to taste
1 cup (250 mL) water

Chicken
2 Tbsp (30 mL) grapeseed oil
2 Tbsp (30 mL) garam masala
    (page 7)
1 Tbsp (15 mL) freshly grated ginger
2 lb (1 kg) boneless, skinless chicken
    breasts, cut into bite-sized pieces

EGG CURRY

IN THE VILLAGE, eggs were considered a kind of meat, and this is why I've included this dish alongside the meat recipes. My next-door neighbor Tikka used to bring fresh egg curry to school, and once in a while he would give me a small taste of his lunch, even though only men and boys were allowed to eat meat. With every bite I felt like I had died and gone to heaven. This dish is inspired by Tikka's curry. *Serves 4*

Eggs are a good source of protein, phosphorus, vitamin B5, vitamin B12, and vitamin D.

2 Tbsp (30 mL) grapeseed oil

1 Tbsp (15 mL) finely chopped ginger

1 Tbsp (15 mL) Tandoori Masala (page 8)

1 tsp (5 mL) ground turmeric

1 tsp (5 mL) ground cumin

1 tsp (5 mL) ground fennel

salt and pepper to taste

1 cup (250 mL) finely chopped tomatoes

1 cup (250 mL) vegetable or chicken broth

1 cup (250 mL) plain yogurt

2 Tbsp (30 mL) chickpea flour

6 eggs

1. **Heat the oil** in a skillet over medium-high heat. When the oil is hot, add the ginger and cook for 15 seconds. Add the Tandoori Masala, turmeric, cumin, fennel, salt, and pepper and cook for 10 seconds. Stir in the tomatoes and cook for 2 minutes. Add the broth and reduce the heat to low.

2. In a small bowl, whisk together the yogurt and the chickpea flour until well mixed. Slowly add the yogurt mixture to the skillet. Turn the heat to high and bring the sauce to a boil. Reduce the heat to low and simmer for 15 minutes.

3. In the meantime, prepare the eggs by placing them in a separate saucepan with enough water to cover. Hard-boil the eggs for about 5 minutes, or a few minutes longer for large eggs. Remove from the heat and allow to cool. Take the eggs out of the pan and peel off the shells, then cut the eggs in half lengthwise and gently place them in the sauce.

4. Serve with rice and Sweet Potatoes in Tamarind Sauce (page 126).

Vegetables, Beans, & Lentils

PATTYPAN SQUASH
WITH SHAVED PARMESAN

PATTYPAN SQUASH IS a summer squash shaped like small discs. It is widely available at South Asian grocery stores (and less so at regular grocery stores). You can find pattypan in green, yellow, and white varieties; I prefer to use the green. Initially this recipe did not include cheese. My daughter, Anoop, sprinkled Parmesan on it, only to discover that Parmesan goes beautifully with cumin! *Serves 4*

2 Tbsp (30 mL) grapeseed oil

2 Tbsp (30 mL) freshly grated ginger

1 Tbsp (15 mL) garam masala (page 7)

1 tsp (5 mL) ground fennel

1 cup (250 mL) halved cherry tomatoes

salt and pepper to taste

1 lb (500 g) pattypan squash, halved lengthwise

¼ cup (60 mL) water

¼ cup (60 mL) freshly shaved Parmesan cheese

1. **Heat the oil** in a skillet over medium-high heat. When the oil is hot, add the ginger and cook for 15 seconds. Add the garam masala and fennel and cook for 10 seconds. Stir in the tomatoes, salt, and pepper. Cook, stirring, for 30 more seconds.

2. Add the squash and water to the skillet. Bring to a boil, then cover with a lid and reduce the heat to medium. Cook for 9 to 12 minutes, or until the squash is tender, stirring regularly. Sprinkle with the cheese.

3. Serve over rice with Chicken Masala with Cherry Tomatoes and Spinach (page 95).

BAKED BABY EGGPLANT
FILLED WITH PANEER

WHEN I VISITED my *masi ji* (my aunt, that is, my mother's sister) in Delhi, I fell in love with her elegant little baby eggplants. When I came back home, I sneaked a few small eggplants from the village garden—even though I wasn't allowed to go anywhere near them since we were supposed to wait to pick them until they were the right size. I created this recipe, placing the eggplants on a pile of burning coals. We didn't have ovens, but I have since discovered that in the oven they turn out even tastier. *Serves 4*

½ lb (250 g) paneer (page 10), crumbled

1 Tbsp (15 mL) cumin seeds

1 Tbsp (15 mL) freshly grated ginger

1 Tbsp (15 mL) coriander seeds, crushed

¼ tsp (1 mL) salt

8 small eggplants

2 Tbsp (30 mL) grapeseed oil

1. **Preheat the oven** to 375°F (190°C).
2. In a large bowl, combine the paneer, cumin seeds, ginger, coriander seeds, and salt and stir until the paneer is well coated with the spices.
3. Cut the eggplants halfway through lengthwise. Scoop out the flesh, chop it finely, and combine it with the paneer mixture.
4. Brush the oil over the eggplant skins. Fill each eggplant with the paneer mixture and place them on a baking tray. Bake for 40 to 50 minutes on the middle rack of the oven.
5. Serve over rice accompanied with Green Pea Soup (page 70).

EGGPLANT WITH COCONUT AND TOMATOES

AFTER I WROTE my first cookbook, I received a lot of email from readers telling me they had not liked eggplant until they tried my eggplant recipes. This has inspired me to write more of them. I'm delighted to be working for this important cause—increasing the number of people who appreciate this purple beauty! *Serves 4*

1. **Heat the oil** in a skillet over medium-high heat. When the oil is hot, add the ginger and cook for 15 seconds. Add the garam masala, mustard seeds, fenugreek seeds, curry leaves, and salt and cook for 10 seconds.
2. Stir in the coconut, tomatoes, eggplant, and water. Bring the mixture to a boil, then reduce the heat to medium-low and cover the skillet with a lid. Simmer until the eggplant is tender, 12 to 15 minutes.
3. Serve with rice and Prawns with Fresh Tomatoes and Yogurt (page 158).

2 Tbsp (30 mL) grapeseed oil

1 Tbsp (15 mL) finely chopped ginger

1 tsp (5 mL) garam masala (page 7)

1 tsp (5 mL) mustard seeds

1 tsp (5 mL) fenugreek seeds

6 to 8 curry leaves

salt to taste

1 cup (250 mL) unsweetened dried coconut flakes

1 cup (250 mL) chopped tomatoes (bite-sized pieces)

1 lb (500 g) eggplant, cut into bite-sized pieces

½ cup (125 mL) water

WHEN A SPECIAL guest from my mother's family would arrive, my mother would go above and beyond to cook the best recipes and serve the best foods possible. This recipe with eggplant and green peas was one of them.

Serves 4

Green peas are a good source of vitamin B6, protein, and fiber.

1. **For the eggplant**, combine all the ingredients, except the eggplant and oil, in a large bowl. Stir well. Heat the oil in a skillet over medium-high heat. Dip the eggplant slices in the batter and place in the skillet. Cook until golden brown on each side, turning frequently so the eggplant does not burn and is cooked through, about 5 to 7 minutes.

2. For the sauce, heat the oil in a saucepan over medium-high heat. When the oil is hot, add the cumin seeds and cook for 10 seconds. Add the frozen peas, water, and salt and bring to a boil. Reduce the heat to low and simmer for 3 minutes, until the peas are tender. Allow to cool.

3. Place the pea mixture in a food processor or blender and purée. Reheat the sauce before serving. Divide the pea mixture into individual bowls and gently place the eggplant slices overtop.

Eggplant

½ cup (125 mL) plain yogurt
½ cup (125 mL) chickpea flour
1 Tbsp (15 mL) lemon juice
1 Tbsp (15 mL) garam masala (page 7)
1 tsp (5 mL) ground fennel
1 tsp (5 mL) ground cardamom
1 tsp (5 mL) Spanish paprika
salt to taste
2 Tbsp (30 mL) grapeseed oil
1 large eggplant, thinly sliced

Green pea sauce

2 Tbsp (30 mL) grapeseed oil
1 tsp (5 mL) cumin seeds
4 cups (1 L) frozen peas
1½ cups (375 mL) water
salt to taste

GREEN BEANS AND PANEER
IN FRESH TOMATO SAUCE

THIS IS ONE of my signature dishes! I cook it often and my kids love it. You can also substitute zucchini or eggplant—in fact, any vegetable you like. This chapter should prove that you really can't go wrong with fresh vegetables and two or three Indian spices. *Serves 4*

Mustard seeds are a very good source of omega-3 fatty acids as well as calcium, zinc, and many other minerals. Mustard is also known to be helpful for digestion and can aid in speeding up metabolism. Who knew that I would learn all that information when I came to North America?

1 Tbsp (15 mL) grapeseed oil

1 tsp (5 mL) finely chopped garlic

1 tsp (5 mL) mustard seeds

1 Tbsp (15 mL) garam masala
   (page 7)

salt and pepper to taste

2 tomatoes, chopped

1 lb (500 g) green beans, trimmed

½ lb (250 g) paneer (page 10),
   cubed and pan-fried

1. **Heat the oil** in a skillet over medium-high heat. When the oil is hot, add the garlic and mustard seeds and cook for 15 seconds. Add the garam masala, salt, and pepper and cook for 5 seconds.
2. Add the tomatoes and green beans and cook, stirring frequently, until the beans are tender, about 7 to 10 minutes. Add the paneer and cook for another 2 minutes before serving.
3. Serve with rice and Maple-Cardamom Salmon (page 153).

112

THIS IS ONE of the many dishes that take me right back to the village, every time. I'd pick green beans from the vine in the garden one by one, remove the tips, and wash them under the hand pump, and I'd also help peel the potatoes.

My mother used only turmeric and garam masala for this recipe. I suggested we add other spices, such as cardamom, mustard seeds, and curry leaves, and my mother thought I was crazy. Even the neighborhood women worried that no one would marry me, creating such strange flavors in the kitchen! I think about this now and can't stop giggling. I hope you will fall in love with this recipe, as many of my North American friends have. *Serves 4*

Green beans contain fiber, protein, calcium, and iron, and are an excellent source of vitamin C.

1. **Heat the oil** in a skillet over medium-high heat. When the oil is hot, add the ginger and cook for 15 seconds. Add the cumin seeds, garam masala, and cardamom and cook for 10 seconds.
2. Add the potatoes, tomatoes, turmeric, salt, and water. Bring to a boil before reducing the heat to medium and covering the skillet with a lid. Simmer, stirring regularly, until the potatoes are almost done, about 9 minutes.
3. Add the beans to the skillet and cook until they are tender, about 5 minutes. Add the yogurt (if using) and stir it in well.
4. Serve with rice and Cod in Tomato Sauce (page 156).

2 Tbsp (30 mL) grapeseed oil
1 Tbsp (15 mL) finely
   chopped ginger
1 Tbsp (15 mL) cumin seeds
1 Tbsp (15 mL) garam masala
   (page 7)
1 tsp (5 mL) ground cardamom
2 cups (500 mL) halved
   small potatoes
1 cup (250 mL) cherry tomatoes
1 tsp (5 mL) ground turmeric
salt to taste
½ cup (125 mL) water
1 lb (500 g) green beans, trimmed
½ cup (125 mL) plain yogurt
   (optional)

Suggested wine

2007 Merlot/Cabernet Sauvignon by Township 7 | A balanced and bold wine with rich, textured flavors of raspberry and blackberry, which pair nicely with the earthy flavor of the cumin seeds and garam masala in this dish.

114

MY AUNT WOULD sometimes make this recipe, and she'd add homemade yogurt to make it creamy. I use sour cream, but of course you can use yogurt too. In my village, potatoes had the stigma of being "poor people's food." Every time I tried potatoes, I found the flavors so warm and welcoming and I wondered why my family did not eat them more often. *Serves 4*

Potatoes are a very good source of vitamin C. They are also a good source of vitamin B6, copper, potassium, manganese, and fiber.

¼ cup (60 mL) grapeseed oil

1 small red onion, finely chopped

1 Tbsp (15 mL) finely chopped ginger

1 Tbsp (15 mL) cumin seeds

1 tsp (5 mL) mustard seeds

1 tsp (5 mL) ground turmeric

1 tsp (5 mL) salt

½ tsp (2 mL) ground cardamom

6 to 8 curry leaves

1 lb (500 g) potatoes, peeled and finely chopped

1 cup (250 mL) low-fat sour cream

1 cup (250 mL) finely chopped tomatoes

1 cup (250 mL) water

1. **Heat the oil** in a skillet over medium-high heat. When the oil is hot, add the onion and ginger and cook for 4 minutes. Add the cumin seeds, mustard seeds, turmeric, salt, cardamom, and curry leaves and cook for 10 seconds.
2. Stir in the potatoes, sour cream, tomatoes, and water, mixing well. Bring the mixture to a boil, then reduce the heat to low and cover with a lid. Simmer, stirring regularly, until the potatoes are tender, about 8 to 10 minutes.
3. Serve with rice or rotis.

116

THIS DISH REMINDS me of the typical lunch we'd have in the village. Lunch was often a vegetable dish, and lentils were something you had as a main dish for dinner. Occasionally, I serve this recipe as a side dish with meat or fish. *Serves 4*

1. **Heat the oil** in a skillet over medium-high heat. When the oil is hot, add the coriander seeds and fenugreek seeds and cook for 5 seconds. Add the ginger and Ginger Masala and cook for 30 seconds. Stir in the tomatoes, turmeric, and salt and cook for another 30 seconds.

2. Stir in the potatoes, frozen mixed vegetables, and water. Bring to a boil, then reduce the heat to low and cover the skillet. Simmer, stirring occasionally, until the potatoes are tender, about 10 minutes.

3. Serve with Spiced Lamb with Mango Sauce (page 84).

2 Tbsp (30 mL) grapeseed oil

1 Tbsp (15 mL) coriander seeds, crushed

1 tsp (5 mL) fenugreek seeds

1 Tbsp (15 mL) finely chopped ginger

1 Tbsp (15 mL) Ginger Masala (page 8)

1 cup (250 mL) chopped tomatoes

1 tsp (5 mL) ground turmeric

1 tsp (5 mL) salt

1 lb (500 g) small red potatoes, halved

1 cup (250 mL) frozen mixed vegetables (peas, corn, and carrots)

¾ cup (185 mL) water

POTATOES OF ALL kinds were quite common in village cooking; paneer was added only on special occasions. This dish is equally delicious if you substitute sweet potatoes (orange- or yellow-fleshed) for white potatoes. This recipe brings aromatic flavors from all over India—garam masala from the north and curry leaves from the south. When I'm away on business and don't have the chance to eat homemade Indian food, this is the dish I miss. *Serves 4*

Curry leaves are known to help with indigestion. **Turmeric** is known for its anti-inflammatory properties.

1. **Heat the oil** in a skillet over medium-high heat. When the oil is hot, add the onion and ginger and cook for 2 minutes. Add the garam masala, turmeric, fenugreek seeds, curry leaves, and salt and cook for 10 seconds. Stir in the tomato paste and cook for another 10 seconds.

2. Add the potatoes, yogurt, and water. Bring the mixture to boil, then reduce the heat to medium-low. Simmer until the potatoes are tender, 12 to 15 minutes. Add the paneer, then remove the skillet from the heat.

3. Serve over rice with Tamarind Scallops (page 162).

3 Tbsp (45 mL) grapeseed oil
1 small onion, finely chopped
1 Tbsp (15 mL) finely chopped ginger
1 Tbsp (15 mL) garam masala (page 7)
1 tsp (5 mL) ground turmeric
1 tsp (5 mL) fenugreek seeds
8 to 10 curry leaves
salt to taste
2 Tbsp (30 mL) tomato paste
5 medium potatoes, peeled and finely chopped
½ cup (125 mL) plain yogurt
3 cups (750 mL) water
1 lb (500 g) paneer (page 10), cut into bite-sized cubes and pan-fried

118

WHEN I MAKE this it's a wonder any snap peas make it into the final dish because I can't stop munching on them while I cook. Maple syrup nicely enhances the already-sweet flavor of the peas. *Serves 4*

Sugar snap peas are a good source of vitamin C, vitamin A, vitamin B2, and vitamin B6. They are also a good source of fiber, protein, niacin, and iron.

2 Tbsp (30 mL) grapeseed oil

1 Tbsp (15 mL) finely
    chopped ginger

1 Tbsp (15 mL) ground coriander

1 Tbsp (15 mL) fennel seeds

1 tsp (5 mL) ground cardamom

salt and pepper to taste

1 lb (500 g) sugar snap peas

¼ cup (60 mL) maple syrup

1. **Heat the oil** in a skillet over medium-high heat. When the oil is hot, add the ginger and cook for 15 seconds. Add the coriander, fennel seeds, cardamom, salt, and pepper and cook for 10 seconds. Stir in the peas and maple syrup and reduce the heat to medium-low. Cook for 6 to 8 minutes, stirring frequently.

2. Serve with rice and Egg Curry (page 103).

MY FIRST INTRODUCTION to the lovely nutty-flavored edamame was in a sushi restaurant. I love taking every chance to use them in my cooking, and I'll even substitute edamame for green peas in a recipe! *Serves 4*

Edamame provide protein and fiber, and of course **tomatoes** are a good source of vitamin C.

1. **Heat the oil** in a skillet on medium-high heat. When the oil is hot, add the ginger and cook for 15 seconds. Add the cumin seeds, mustard seeds, and coriander seeds and cook for 10 seconds.
2. Add the edamame, tomatoes, turmeric, and salt to the skillet. Cook until the beans are tender, 3 to 5 minutes.
3. Serve with rice and Spiced Lamb with Coconut Sauce (page 83).

2 Tbsp (30 mL) grapeseed oil
1 tsp (5 mL) finely chopped ginger
1 tsp (5 mL) cumin seeds
1 tsp (5 mL) mustard seeds
1 tsp (5 mL) coriander seeds, crushed
1 lb (500 g) frozen shelled edamame
1 cup (250 mL) finely chopped tomatoes
1 tsp (5 mL) ground turmeric
salt to taste

KIDNEY BEANS WITH
BLUEBERRY SAUCE

THIS COMBINATION OF blueberries and spicy beans was something I discovered by chance. I was looking for tomato paste in the refrigerator and realized I had some leftover blueberry sauce from a dessert I had made the night before. I decided to use the blueberry sauce instead just to see how it would go with Indian spices, and the result went beyond my expectations! *Serves 4*

Blueberries are a very good source of vitamin C and vitamin E. They also contain high amounts of antioxidants.

2 Tbsp (30 mL) grapeseed oil

1 Tbsp (15 mL) finely chopped garlic

1 Tbsp (15 mL) cumin seeds

1 Tbsp (15 mL) coriander seeds, crushed

1 Tbsp (15 mL) garam masala (page 7)

6 to 8 curry leaves

salt to taste

1 cup (250 mL) whole cherry tomatoes

1 cup (250 mL) blueberries, fresh or frozen

14 oz (398 mL) can kidney beans, drained and rinsed

1. **Heat the oil** in a skillet on medium-high heat. When the oil is hot, add the garlic, cumin seeds, coriander seeds, garam masala, curry leaves, and salt and cook for 10 seconds.
2. Stir in the tomatoes and blueberries. Turn the heat to medium-low and cook until the blueberries are tender, about 5 to 7 minutes. Add the kidney beans and cook for 2 more minutes, then turn the heat off.
3. Serve over rice accompanied with Indian Rice Flake Salad (page 24).

SIMPLE CHICKPEAS

ON DAYS WHEN I do not feel like doing any major cooking but still want to serve something nutritious and tasty, I make this. Trust me, this recipe is magic. The highlight of this dish is the fresh ginger, which I always have in my fridge. You should, too! *Serves 4*

Ginger has long been used as a natural treatment for colds and the flu, and **turmeric** is known for its anti-inflammatory properties.

2 Tbsp (30 mL) grapeseed oil
1 Tbsp (15 mL) finely
    chopped ginger
1 Tbsp (15 mL) cumin seeds
1 Tbsp (15 mL) garam masala
    (page 7)
1 tsp (5 mL) ground turmeric
salt to taste
19 oz (540 mL) can chickpeas,
    drained and rinsed
2 Tbsp (30 mL) plain yogurt

1. **Heat the oil** in a skillet over medium-high heat. When the oil is hot, add the ginger and cook for 15 seconds. Add the cumin seeds, garam masala, turmeric, and salt and cook for 20 seconds. Stir in the chickpeas and yogurt, reduce the heat to medium-low, and cook for 3 minutes.
2. Serve over rice with Grilled Chicken in Yogurt (page 91).

SWEET AND SOUR CHICKPEAS

INTRODUCING SWEET AND sour flavors to a chickpea dish was an experiment, so I was delighted this turned out to be a big hit. Anoop loves it when I pack this for her school lunch. Vegetarian dishes are her favorite, and I love the challenge of packing as much flavor into them as possible!

Maybe someday I will tell my kids that as soon as I know they love a recipe, I start sneaking in just a few more spices. Not only do I want to expand their palate, I want them to benefit from the amazing health properties always being discovered in spices. *Serves 4*

Coriander is a good source of fiber, iron, and magnesium, and can aid in lowering bad cholesterol (LDL) and raising good cholesterol (HDL).

2 Tbsp (30 mL) grapeseed oil

1 small red onion, finely chopped

1 Tbsp (15 mL) finely chopped ginger

1 Tbsp (15 mL) mustard seeds

1 Tbsp (15 mL) ground coriander

10 to 12 curry leaves

salt to taste

19 oz (540 mL) can chickpeas, drained and rinsed

½ cup (125 mL) mango juice

2 Tbsp (30 mL) tamarind pulp (page 8)

1. **Heat the oil** in a skillet over medium-high heat. When the oil is hot, add the onion and ginger and cook for 2 minutes. Add the mustard seeds, coriander, curry leaves, and salt and cook for 10 seconds.

2. Stir in the chickpeas, mango juice, and tamarind pulp. Reduce the heat to medium-low and cook for 2 more minutes before serving.

3. Serve over rice with Squash and Papaya Soup on the side (page 71).

IN MY KITCHEN I cook with lentils, chickpeas, and beans very frequently. There is really no end to what you can do with them. The best part of this recipe is that the spices form a nice crust on the sweet potatoes. *Serves 4*

1. **To prepare the lentils**, place all the ingredients in a saucepan and bring to a boil. Turn the heat to low and simmer until the lentils are soft, about 15 to 18 minutes.

2. To prepare the spiced sweet potatoes, heat the oil in a skillet over medium-high heat. When the oil is hot, add the ginger and cook for 10 seconds. Add the cumin seeds, Ginger Masala, coriander seeds, mustard seeds, curry leaves, and salt and cook for 5 seconds. Stir in the sweet potato and water. Bring to a boil and turn the heat to low and simmer, stirring regularly, until the sweet potato is tender, about 12 to 15 minutes.

3. To serve, add the cooked sweet potatoes to the lentils and mix them gently. Enjoy over rice or with rotis.

Lentils

3 cups (750 mL) split red lentils (*masoor dhal*)

6 cups (1.5 L) water

½ tsp (2 mL) salt

1 tsp (5 mL) ground turmeric

Spiced sweet potatoes

2 Tbsp (30 mL) grapeseed oil

1 Tbsp (15 mL) finely chopped ginger

1 Tbsp (15 mL) cumin seeds

1 Tbsp (15 mL) Ginger Masala (page 8)

½ tsp (2 mL) coriander seeds, crushed

½ tsp (2 mL) mustard seeds

10 to 12 curry leaves

⅛ tsp (0.5 mL) salt

1 small sweet potato, peeled and cubed

½ cup (125 mL) water

126

IN THE VILLAGE, tamarind was used only to make chutneys. When I came to Canada I started incorporating tamarind into other dishes. If you do not have tamarind, use ¼ cup (60 mL) of sundried tomatoes instead. They are just as rich and tangy and will go with the spices cumin and coriander. *Serves 4*

1. **Heat the oil** in a skillet over medium-high heat. When the oil is hot, add the onion, garlic, and ginger and cook for 3 minutes, stirring regularly. Add the cumin seeds, coriander seeds, and garam masala and cook for 10 seconds.

2. Stir in the sweet potatoes, tamarind pulp, and brown sugar. Add the vegetable broth and bring to a boil. Turn the heat to low, cover the pot with a lid, and simmer until the sweet potatoes are tender, 12 to 15 minutes.

3. Serve with rice and Grilled Chicken with Coriander (page 90).

3 Tbsp (45 mL) grapeseed oil

1 small onion, thinly sliced

1 Tbsp (15 mL) finely chopped garlic

1 Tbsp (15 mL) finely chopped ginger

1 Tbsp (15 mL) cumin seeds

1 Tbsp (15 mL) coriander seeds, crushed

1 Tbsp (15 mL) garam masala (page 7)

1 lb (500 g) sweet potatoes, peeled and cubed

¼ cup (60 mL) tamarind pulp (page 8)

1 Tbsp (15 mL) brown sugar

2 cups (500 mL) vegetable broth

EGGPLANT AND SWEET POTATOES WITH CHERRY TOMATOES

THE SWEETNESS OF sweet potatoes and the earthiness of eggplant make a great combination, but this recipe is far from traditional. Doing anything nontraditional in the kitchen, like using slightly different ingredients, would always annoy my elders! But now that I am in North America, I can be as wild as I want. I love being creative, and exploring and having fun with ingredients.

Serves 4

2 Tbsp (30 mL) grapeseed oil

1 Tbsp (15 mL) finely grated
   fresh ginger

1 Tbsp (15 mL) cumin seeds

1 Tbsp (15 mL) garam masala
   (page 7)

1 tsp (5 mL) ground turmeric

salt to taste

1 lb (500 g) sweet potatoes,
   peeled and finely chopped

1 lb (500 g) eggplant, cut into
   bite-sized pieces

1 cup (250 mL) halved
   cherry tomatoes

½ cup (125 mL) water

1. **Heat the oil** in a skillet over medium-high heat. When the oil is hot, add the ginger and cook for 15 seconds. Add the cumin seeds, garam masala, turmeric, and salt and cook for 10 seconds.

2. Add the sweet potatoes, eggplant, tomatoes, and water to the skillet. Reduce the heat to medium and cook, stirring regularly, until the sweet potatoes and eggplant are tender, about 16 to 20 minutes.

3. Serve with rice and Prawns with Cardamom and Fennel (page 159).

CURRIED PUMPKIN

ONE OF MY jobs as a child was to remove the seeds from the pumpkin before my mom could cook with it. When I was a bit older, I started saving the seeds and drying them in the sun, and I'd toast them in an iron pan over the barbecue pit. Cooking often brings up sweet, innocent memories from childhood for me! *Serves 4*

Pumpkins are full of beta-carotene and potassium rich.

1. **Heat the oil** in a skillet over medium-high heat. When the oil is hot, add the onion and ginger and cook for 2 minutes. Stir in the tomatoes, fenugreek seeds, garam masala, and salt and cook for 5 minutes.
2. Add the pumpkin, vegetable broth and chili to the skillet. Bring to a boil, then reduce the heat to low. Cook until the pumpkin is tender, 15 to 18 minutes.
3. Serve over rice.

3 Tbsp (45 mL) grapeseed oil
1 small onion, finely chopped
1 tsp (5 mL) finely chopped ginger
1 cup (250 mL) finely chopped tomatoes
1 Tbsp (15 mL) fenugreek seeds
1 tsp (5 mL) garam masala (page 7)
salt to taste
1 lb (500 g) pumpkin, seeded, peeled, and cubed
½ cup (125 mL) vegetable broth
1 medium green chili, finely sliced

THIS IS A simple gourmet dish that will impress your guests—mustard seeds and cumin blended with cream cheese and wine to create a tasty sauce for sweet potatoes. I like to use Pinot Grigio, but you can use any white wine you prefer. *Serves 4*

Sweet potatoes are a good source of fiber, potassium, vitamin C, manganese, and vitamin B6.

1. **Heat the oil** in a skillet over medium-high heat. When the oil is hot, add the ginger and cook for 15 seconds. Add the mustard seeds and cumin seeds and cook for 10 seconds. Add the wine, cream cheese, and salt, stirring gently to combine.
2. Stir the sweet potatoes into the sauce. Bring to a boil, then reduce the heat to medium-low and cover. Simmer until the sweet potatoes are tender, about 12 to 15 minutes.
3. Serve with rotis or rice.

2 Tbsp (30 mL) grapeseed oil
1 Tbsp (15 mL) finely chopped ginger
1 tsp (5 mL) mustard seeds
1 tsp (5 mL) cumin seeds
½ cup (125 mL) white wine
¼ cup (60 mL) cream cheese
salt to taste
1 lb (500 g) sweet potatoes, peeled and cut into ½-inch (1 cm) cubes

MY MOTHER ALWAYS cooked squash with fenugreek seeds. Without them I could tell that something was missing. Here I also use cilantro, which gives the squash yet another distinct flavor. *Serves 4*

1. **Heat the oil** in a skillet over medium-high heat. When the oil is hot, add the onion and chilies and cook for 3 minutes. Add the fenugreek seeds, garam masala, turmeric, salt, and pepper and cook for 10 seconds.
2. Stir in the squash, tomatoes, water, and cilantro (if using). Bring the mixture to a boil, then reduce the heat to medium-low and cook until the squash is tender, 12 to 15 minutes.
3. Serve with rice and Tamarind Scallops (page 162).

2 Tbsp (30 mL) grapeseed oil

1 small onion, finely chopped

2 green chilies, finely chopped

1 Tbsp (15 mL) fenugreek seeds

1 Tbsp (15 mL) garam masala (page 7)

1 tsp (5 mL) ground turmeric

salt and pepper to taste

1 lb (500 g) banana squash, peeled and chopped into bite-sized pieces

1 cup (250 mL) finely chopped tomatoes

¼ cup (60 mL) water

2 Tbsp (30 mL) finely chopped cilantro (optional)

MY MOTHER USED to make this often, except her version used red onions and ginger in addition to all the spices here, and she'd cut the carrot into big chunks instead of ribbons. Occasionally she'd grate it and also add peas. My daughter now loves this dish. She helps me prepare it, just like I helped my mother in the kitchen.

Serves 4

Carrots are a rich source of vitamins A and C.

1. **Heat the oil** in a skillet over medium-high heat. When the oil is hot, add the ginger and cook for 15 seconds. Add the garam masala, mustard seeds, coriander, and curry leaves and cook for 10 seconds.
2. Add the peas to the skillet, then reduce the heat to medium and cook until the peas are tender, about 3 to 5 minutes. Add the carrots and salt and turn the heat off. Serve immediately.
3. Serve with Chickpea Flour Roti (page 172).

2 Tbsp (30 mL) grapeseed oil
1 Tbsp (15 mL) finely chopped ginger
1 Tbsp (15 mL) garam masala (page 7)
1 tsp (5 mL) mustard seeds
1 tsp (5 mL) ground coriander
10 to 12 curry leaves
2 cups (500 mL) frozen or fresh peas
½ lb (250 g) carrots, peeled then sliced into ribbons using a vegetable peeler
salt to taste

Suggested wine

2008 Malbec by Red Rooster
This full-bodied wine is rich with fig, blueberry, plum, and black cherry flavors, and complements the toasted mustard seeds and curry leaves.

CABBAGE WHEN COOKED can become nice and soft, even mushy, and I like adding chickpeas for contrast. Then again, I am obsessed with chickpeas and would add them to just about anything. *Serves 4*

Cabbage is a very good source of fiber and omega-3 fatty acids. It also contains calcium, potassium, magnesium, vitamin A, and protein.

1 Tbsp (15 mL) grapeseed oil

1 Tbsp (15 mL) finely
    chopped ginger

1 Tbsp (15 mL) garam masala
    (page 7)

1 Tbsp (15 mL) fenugreek seeds

1 tsp (5 mL) cumin seeds

1 tsp (5 mL) ground turmeric

salt to taste

1 small head of cabbage,
    thinly chopped

1 cup (250 mL) finely
    chopped tomatoes

¼ cup (60 mL) water

14 oz (398 mL) can chickpeas,
    drained and rinsed

1. **Heat the oil** in a skillet on medium-high heat. When the oil is hot, add the ginger, garam masala, fenugreek seeds, cumin seeds, turmeric, and salt and cook for 15 seconds.

2. Add the cabbage, tomatoes, and water to the skillet. Reduce the heat to medium-low and cover the skillet with a lid. Cook until the cabbage is tender, 10 to 15 minutes. Add the chickpeas and cook for 2 more minutes.

3. Enjoy with rotis and Rice with Edamame (page 168).

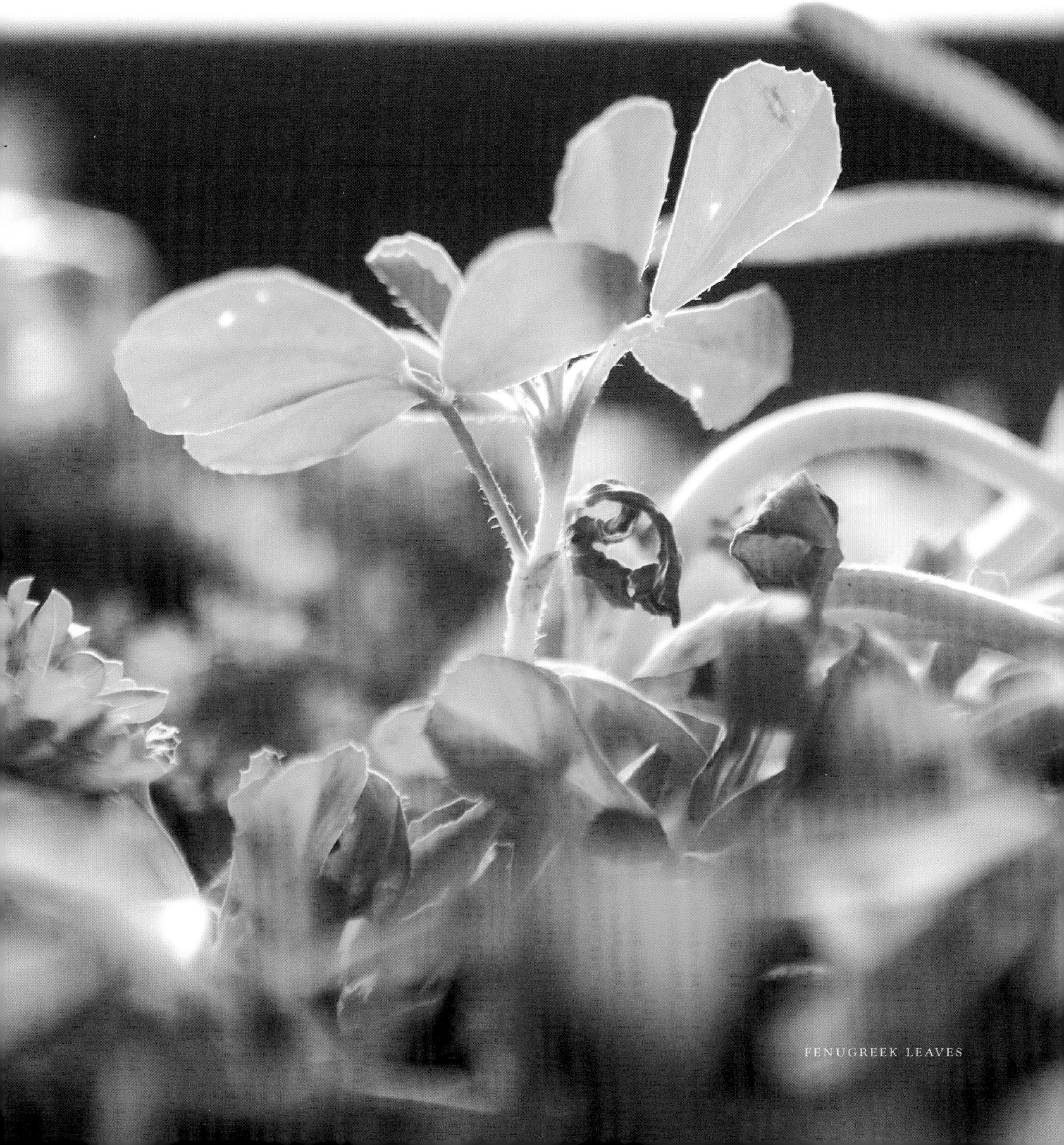

FENUGREEK LEAVES

PANEER BALLS

I HAD THIS dish for the first time when I was visiting my uncle and his family in Delhi, where the food was very different from what I was used to in the village. Here's a healthier version using yogurt instead of cream.

Serves 4

1. **Combine all the ingredients** except the oil in a large bowl. Stir well until the spices are evenly distributed. Using your hands, roll the mixture into spheres about the size of golf balls.
2. Heat the oil in a nonstick pan over medium-high heat. When the oil is hot, gently place the paneer balls in the pan and cook, turning frequently, until the balls are golden brown on all sides, about 4 to 7 minutes.
3. Serve with rice and Scallops with Tomatoes and Papaya (page 160).

1 cup (250 mL) crumbled paneer (page 10)
¼ cup (60 mL) chickpea flour
¼ cup (60 mL) plain yogurt
1 Tbsp (15 mL) finely grated fresh ginger
1 Tbsp (15 mL) dried fenugreek leaves
1 Tbsp (15 mL) cumin seeds
1 Tbsp (15 mL) ground coriander
¼ tsp (1 mL) Spanish paprika
salt to taste
2 Tbsp (30 mL) grapeseed oil

SCRAMBLED PANEER
AND ASPARAGUS

I WAS RAISED vegetarian, almost vegan—eggs were considered meat. I was so curious about the taste of eggs that many times I secretly exchanged my lunch at school with another student's scrambled eggs. And after all that, I now prefer making scramble using paneer! *Serves 4*

I added **asparagus** to the recipe because it not only tastes great but is a good source of fiber, protein, and vitamin C.

1. **Heat the oil** in a skillet over medium-high heat. When the oil is hot, add the ginger, cumin seeds, mustard seeds, and curry leaves and cook for 20 seconds. Add the paneer, turmeric, paprika, salt, and pepper. Reduce the heat to medium and cook for 2 minutes, stirring regularly. Add the asparagus and cook for 3 to 5 minutes.
2. Serve with rice and Chicken with Almond Butter (page 96).

2 Tbsp (30 mL) grapeseed oil

1 Tbsp (15 mL) finely chopped ginger

1 Tbsp (15 mL) cumin seeds

1 tsp (5 mL) mustard seeds

6 to 8 curry leaves

1 lb (500 g) paneer (page 10), crumbled

½ tsp (2 mL) ground turmeric

¼ tsp (1 mL) Spanish paprika

salt and pepper to taste

1 lb (500 g) asparagus, ends snapped off and spears cut in half

TAMARIND MUSHROOMS

SOMETIMES I USE these mushrooms in a roti wrap, and sometimes as a stuffing for turkey. The mushrooms and spices add delicious flavors to turkey as it bakes (and if it's a concern, the whole thing is gluten free!). *Serves 4*

Mushrooms are an excellent source of potassium and riboflavin.

1. **Heat the oil** in a skillet over medium-high heat. When the oil is hot, add the ginger, garam masala, turmeric, mustard seeds, cumin seeds, salt, and pepper and cook for 10 seconds. Add the mushrooms and tamarind pulp. Reduce the heat to medium and cook, stirring frequently, until the mushrooms are tender, 9 to 12 minutes.
2. Serve with rotis and Ginger and Coconut Chicken (page 100).

2 Tbsp (30 mL) grapeseed oil

1 Tbsp (15 mL) finely grated fresh ginger

1 Tbsp (15 mL) garam masala (page 7)

1 tsp (5 mL) ground turmeric

1 tsp (5 mL) mustard seeds

1 tsp (5 mL) cumin seeds

salt and pepper to taste

1 lb (500 g) button mushrooms, finely chopped

2 Tbsp (30 mL) tamarind pulp (page 8)

VILLAGE-STYLE PORTOBELLO MUSHROOMS

PORTOBELLO MUSHROOMS HAVE a hearty flavor matched by garam masala. This dish works both as a side and as a main meal (with brown rice). *Serves 4*

There are many naturally occurring antioxidants in **portobello mushrooms**, and they are rich in minerals such as copper and potassium.

1 Tbsp (15 mL) grapeseed oil
1 Tbsp (15 mL) finely chopped garlic
1 Tbsp (15 mL) garam masala (page 7)
1 tsp (5 mL) mustard seeds
1 lb (500 g) portobello mushrooms, sliced
1 cup (250 mL) frozen peas
1 cup (250 mL) chopped tomatoes
1 cup (250 mL) vegetable broth

1. **Heat the oil** in a skillet over medium-high heat. When the oil is hot, add the garlic, garam masala, and mustard seeds and cook over medium heat for 20 seconds. Add the mushrooms, peas, and tomatoes and cook for 2 minutes.
2. Add the vegetable broth to the skillet. Bring to a boil and then reduce the heat to low. Cover the skillet with a lid and cook for 5 to 7 minutes.
3. Serve on brown rice and/or with Chicken Thighs with Tomatoes and Eggplant (page 101).

SHIITAKE MUSHROOMS WITH FENNEL SEEDS

I MUST HAVE been in my teens when my father first brought white mushrooms home from the city. He was a baptized Sikh and not eating any meat at the time. As someone who missed chicken, he was excited to have found a vegetable with a similar texture. My brother agreed it was a good substitute, but frankly I couldn't understand what they were talking about!

It is now very common for shiitake mushrooms to act as a stand-in for meat. Shiitakes are more of a substantial mushroom, but I am starting to see why mushrooms are considered "meaty." I love shiitake's texture and taste, but of course you can use any mushroom you desire.

Serves 4

Shiitake mushrooms are a very good source of zinc, copper, and selenium and contain protein, fiber, and vitamin B6.

2 Tbsp (30 mL) grapeseed oil
1 Tbsp (15 mL) finely
    chopped ginger
1 Tbsp (15 mL) fennel seeds
1 tsp (5 mL) coriander seeds,
    crushed
1 lb (500 g) shiitake mushrooms,
    thinly sliced
1 tsp (5 mL) ground turmeric
salt and pepper to taste

1. **Heat the oil** in a skillet on medium-high heat. When the oil is hot, add the ginger, fennel seeds, and coriander seeds and cook for 30 seconds. Add the mushrooms, turmeric, salt, and pepper, then reduce the heat to low and cover. Cook, stirring regularly, until the mushrooms are tender, about 9 to 12 minutes.
2. Serve with rice and Fenugreek Chicken (page 97).

142

OKRA HAS A unique flavor and interesting texture. I prefer to serve it with a minimal sauce; okra can become more slimy when it is cooked with too much liquid. *Serves 4*

Okra is a good source of many nutrients, including vitamins B6 and C, fiber, calcium, and folate.

1. **Heat the oil** in a skillet over medium-high heat. When the oil is hot, add the coriander seeds and garam masala and cook for 10 seconds. Add the okra, onion, and salt. Reduce the heat to medium and cook, stirring regularly, until the okra is tender, about 12 to 14 minutes.
2. Fill a saucepan with water and bring to a boil. Add the egg noodles and cook until the noodles have reached the desired level of tenderness, about 3 to 5 minutes. Drain the noodles and serve topped with the okra.

2 Tbsp (30 mL) grapeseed oil

1 Tbsp (15 mL) coriander seeds, crushed

1 Tbsp (15 mL) garam masala (page 7)

1 lb (500 g) okra, hard ends removed, cut in chunks

1 medium onion, finely chopped

salt to taste

5 oz (150 g) package egg noodles

Suggested wine

2008 Muscat Ottonel by Hillside Estate | I had never tried 100 percent Muscat Ottonel before, and I was pleasantly surprised at how well it paired with the coriander and garam masala in this recipe.

144

WHEN I WARM up these vegetables at work, my colleagues line up at my office for a taste. I think it's mostly the warm and earthy aroma of cumin. This is a great way to get your vegetables! *Serves 4*

Baby corn is rich in vitamin C, **carrots** are an excellent source of antioxidants, **broccoli** contains vitamins K, C, and A, and **cauliflower** is a good source of vitamin C and fiber.

1. **Heat the oil** in a skillet over medium-high heat. When the oil is hot, add the ginger, fennel seeds, cumin seeds, garam masala, turmeric, salt, and pepper and cook for 10 seconds. Reduce the heat to medium. Add the broccoli, cauliflower, baby corn, and carrots and cook until the carrots have softened, about 5 minutes.
2. Serve with rice and Traditional Chicken with Spinach Sauce (page 102).

2 Tbsp (30 mL) grapeseed oil
1 Tbsp (15 mL) finely
   chopped ginger
1 Tbsp (15 mL) fennel seeds
1 Tbsp (15 mL) cumin seeds
1 Tbsp (15 mL) garam masala
   (page 7)
1 tsp (5 mL) ground turmeric
salt and pepper to taste
2 cups (500 mL) broccoli florets
2 cups (500 mL) cauliflower florets
1 cup (250 mL) baby corn, chopped
1 cup (250 mL) thinly sliced
   peeled carrots

GRILLED MUSHROOMS, ASPARAGUS, AND RED PEPPER WITH TOFU

MY FIRST TASTE of tofu was when I was a young girl and my grandma, who lived in London, England, came to visit me in the village. She went to the city and bought tofu and made us tofu curry. I was hooked; I immediately loved the flavor and texture of tofu.

Asparagus, mushrooms, red pepper, and tofu provide contrasting textures and colors, and a little honey adds a touch of sweetness. We often eat this as a main dish, and—because the dish is so attractive looking—as a side dish when guests come over. *Serves 4*

Tofu is high in protein and a good source of iron.

¼ cup (60 mL) grapeseed oil
¼ cup (60 mL) balsamic vinegar
1 Tbsp (15 mL) liquid honey
1 Tbsp (15 mL) ground cumin
1 Tbsp (15 mL) finely chopped garlic
1 Tbsp (15 mL) ground coriander
½ tsp (2 mL) salt
¼ tsp (1 mL) pepper
4 large portobello mushrooms, sliced
2 red peppers, chopped into large pieces
1 lb (500 g) asparagus, ends snapped off and spears cut in half
10 oz (300 g) extra-firm tofu, cut into 2-inch (5 cm) cubes

1. **Preheat the barbecue** to medium-high heat, or if you prefer to use the oven, preheat it to 375°F (190°C).
2. In a large bowl, combine the oil, balsamic vinegar, honey, cumin, garlic, coriander, salt, and pepper and mix well. Add the mushrooms, red peppers, asparagus, and tofu and toss until the spices are evenly distributed.
3. Cut a sheet of foil large enough to completely enclose the vegetables. Place the vegetables on the foil and fold it over to cover the vegetables.
4. Lower the heat of the barbecue to medium and cook the vegetables on the top rack for 12 to 15 minutes. Alternatively, bake the vegetables in the oven, wrapped in foil, for 25 minutes.
5. Serve with rice.

PAN-FRIED TOFU SERVED ON STEAMED SPINACH

MY DAUGHTER, ANOOP, loves this dish and enjoys making it herself. This warm and earthy blend of spices has a nice hint of licorice flavor. Anoop may not be able to identify each spice by its aroma and taste, but I have heard her say that she loves those aromas and could not live without them—sweet music to my ears since I grew up loving those very same spices. *Serves 4*

2 Tbsp (30 mL) grapeseed oil
1 lb (500 g) extra-firm tofu,
    cut in slices
½ tsp (2 mL) ground cardamom
½ tsp (2 mL) ground fennel
¼ tsp (1 mL) ground cumin
¼ tsp (1 mL) ground coriander
salt to taste
1 lb (500 g) fresh spinach

1. **Heat the oil** in a skillet over medium-high heat. When the oil is hot, place the tofu slices in the skillet and brown them on both sides.
2. While the tofu is browning, combine the cardamom, fennel, cumin, coriander, and salt in a small bowl. Sprinkle the spice mixture over the tofu. Turn the heat off and cover the skillet with a lid.
3. Rinse the spinach and place it in a vegetable steamer, or place it in a large saucepan with a few tablespoons of water and set it over medium heat. Steam the spinach until the leaves wilt just a little, about 3 to 4 minutes. Drain the spinach in a colander to remove excess water.
4. Divide the spinach among 4 plates and arrange the tofu slices overtop. Serve.

BITTER MELON, ALSO known as bitter gourd, is in the same family as cucumber, melon, squash, and pumpkins. It looks like a cucumber with bumps all over it, and you can find it at Indian grocery stores. Its bitter flavor is nicely complemented by fenugreek seeds and coriander. In the village there were only two ways to cook bitter melon: stuffed with onions and cooked in oil over low heat; or with paneer, as I have done here. *Serves 4*

Bitter melon is rich in iron and calcium, contains more beta-carotene than broccoli, and has twice the potassium of a banana.

1. **Heat the oil** in a skillet over medium-high heat. When the oil is hot, add the fennel seeds, coriander, fenugreek, salt, and pepper and cook for 10 seconds. Stir in the onion and ginger, reduce the heat to medium, and cook for 2 minutes.
2. Add the paneer to the skillet and cook for 3 minutes, then stir in the bitter melon and tomatoes. Turn the heat to low and cook, stirring frequently, for 12 minutes.
3. Serve over rice.

147

2 Tbsp (30 mL) grapeseed oil
1 Tbsp (15 mL) fennel seeds
1 Tbsp (15 mL) ground coriander
½ tsp (2 mL) ground fenugreek (seeds)
salt and pepper to taste
1 small onion, thinly sliced
1 Tbsp (15 mL) finely grated fresh ginger
1 lb (500 g) paneer (page 10), crumbled
1 lb (500 g) bitter melon, peeled, seeds discarded, and flesh finely chopped
1 cup (250 mL) finely chopped tomatoes

Fish & Seafood

150

GROUND SPICES CREATE a very aromatic crust for the salmon. Add green beans as an accompaniment and you have a perfect salmon dish. *Serves 4*

1. **Preheat the barbecue** to medium heat.
2. In a small bowl, combine the cumin, fenugreek, and fennel. Rub the spice mixture on the salmon. Grill the salmon until it begins to flake with a fork, about 12 to 14 minutes.
3. While the salmon is grilling, heat the oil in a skillet over medium-high heat. When the oil is hot, add the fennel seeds and ginger and cook for 10 seconds. Stir in the beans and cook until they are still slightly crunchy, 5 to 7 minutes. Add the sesame seeds, salt, and pepper.
4. Divide the salmon into 4 portions. Distribute the beans among 4 plates and serve the salmon over the cooked beans. Garnish with sunflower sprouts.

Salmon

1 tsp (5 mL) ground cumin
½ tsp (2 mL) ground fenugreek (seeds)
½ tsp (2 mL) ground fennel
1 lb (500 g) salmon fillet(s)

Green beans

2 Tbsp (30 mL) grapeseed oil
1 Tbsp (15 mL) fennel seeds
1 tsp (5 mL) finely chopped ginger
1 lb (500 g) green beans, trimmed
1 tsp (5 mL) sesame seeds
salt and pepper to taste
sunflower sprouts for garnish

Suggested wine

2007 Pinot Noir by Howling Bluff | The pungent flavors of ginger and fennel bring out this Pinot Noir's raspberry and cherry notes and undertones of smoky bacon.

152

THIS IS A very fine gourmet dish that can be beautifully presented and will certainly impress your guests. It's also easy to put together—but your guests don't have to know that. *Serves 4*

Salmon is low in calories yet high in protein and a perfect source of omega-3 essential fatty acids.

1. **Preheat the oven** to 375°F (190°C).
2. Combine the lentils, water, garam masala, turmeric, and salt in a saucepan over medium-high heat and bring to a boil. Reduce the heat to low and cook until the lentils are tender, about 20 minutes.
3. While the lentils are cooking, prepare the salmon. Combine the yogurt, chickpea flour, cumin, and fenugreek leaves in a large bowl, mixing well. Dip each salmon fillet in the yogurt mixture to coat all sides.
4. Heat the oil in an ovenproof saucepan over medium-high heat. When the oil is hot, gently place the coated salmon in the pan and sear until brown on both sides, about 2 minutes per side. Place the pan on the middle rack of the oven and cook until the salmon flakes easily with a fork, about 7 to 9 minutes.
5. To serve, spoon the lentils into 4 large dinner bowls and top each serving with a piece of salmon.

1 cup (250 mL) yellow lentils (*chana dhal*)

5 cups (1.25 L) water

1 Tbsp (15 mL) garam masala (page 7)

1 tsp (5 mL) ground turmeric

½ tsp (2 mL) salt

½ cup (125 mL) plain yogurt

2 Tbsp (30 mL) chickpea flour

1 Tbsp (15 mL) ground cumin

1 Tbsp (15 mL) dried fenugreek leaves

4 salmon fillets, about ½ lb (250 g) each

2 Tbsp (30 mL) grapeseed oil

MAPLE-CARDAMOM SALMON

I LOVE MAPLE syrup and enjoy cooking with it. Barbecuing salmon fillets brushed with maple syrup and spices results in something that may remind you of salmon candy. This recipe calls for bok choy, but asparagus or spinach can be used instead. *Serves 4*

Not only is **maple syrup** tasty and sweet, it is also a good source of manganese and zinc.

1. **Preheat the barbecue** to medium heat.
2. In a small bowl, combine the maple syrup, cardamom, and paprika, mixing well. Brush each side of the salmon fillets with the mixture. Gently place the salmon directly on the grill. Cook until it flakes easily, about 12 to 15 minutes.
3. Heat the oil in a skillet over medium-high heat. When the oil is hot, add the cumin seeds and ginger and cook for 20 seconds. Add the bok choy and water. Reduce the heat to low and cover with a lid. Cook the bok choy until it starts wilting, about 3 minutes. Sprinkle with the lemon zest.
4. Divide the bok choy equally among 4 plates. Cut each salmon fillet in half and arrange over the bok choy. Enjoy!

¼ cup (60 mL) maple syrup
1 Tbsp (15 mL) ground cardamom
1 tsp (5 mL) Spanish paprika
2 salmon fillets, about ½ lb (250 g) each
1 Tbsp (15 mL) grapeseed oil
1 tsp (5 mL) cumin seeds
1 tsp (5 mL) finely grated fresh ginger
2 lb (1 kg) bok choy
¼ cup (60 mL) water
1 tsp (5 mL) lemon zest

CORIANDER TUNA
WITH BROCCOLINI

I LOVE THE look of freshly seared tuna. And the only spice I use is coriander seed, a delicious flavor that will linger with each bite. This is a feast for your eyes as well as your palate. *Serves 4*

1. **Sprinkle the coriander seeds** on a plate. Gently dip the top side and the bottom side of the tuna in the coriander.

2. Heat 2 Tbsp (30 mL) of the oil in a skillet over medium-high heat. When the oil is hot, turn the heat down to medium. Place the tuna in the pan and sear on one side for about 10 to 15 seconds, until it is crisp and golden brown, then flip and sear the other side. The tuna should be rare in the middle. Set aside.

3. Place the broccolini in a vegetable steamer, or in a large saucepan filled with boiling water. Steam until the stems are crisp-tender, about 5 minutes. Drain in a colander, then rinse with cold water to stop it from overcooking. Drain again.

4. Heat 1 Tbsp (15 mL) of the oil in a skillet over medium-high heat. Add mustard seeds, steamed broccolini, and salt to taste and sauté for 1 minute.

5. Serve the seared tuna with the broccolini on the side. Enjoy!

¼ cup (60 mL) coriander seeds, crushed
½ lb (250 g) fresh tuna fillet
3 Tbsp (45 mL) grapeseed oil (divided)
1 lb (500 g) broccolini
1 tsp (5 mL) mustard seeds

Suggested wine

2007 Portfolio by Laughing Stock Vineyards | I love Bordeaux varietals, and this one has all of my favorite grapes: Merlot, Cabernet Sauvignon, Cabernet Franc, Malbec, and Petit Verdot. The wine's candied cherry, blackberry, and dark chocolate tones combined with the toasty coriander in this recipe is magic to my palate.

COD IN TOMATO SAUCE

I OFTEN COOK this when Anoop's friends come for dinner. Tender, flaky cod in a lightly spiced tomato sauce—so simple and so elegant. Anoop's friends have said it's the best way they've ever had cod and I know they weren't just saying it to be polite! *Serves 4*

Cod is an excellent low-calorie source of protein and a good source of omega-3 fatty acids. It also contains vitamins B12 and B6.

1. **Preheat the barbecue** to medium heat. Gently place the cod directly on the grill and cook it until it is fully cooked and flakes easily, about 10 to 12 minutes. Remove from the grill, carefully cut it into cubes, and set it aside.
2. While the cod is cooking, prepare the tomato sauce. Heat the oil in a skillet over medium-high heat. When the oil is hot, add the garlic, cumin seeds, coriander, mustard seeds, fennel, paprika, curry leaves, salt, and pepper and cook for 20 seconds. Stir in the tomato paste and cook for an additional 10 seconds.
3. Stir the crushed tomatoes and vegetable broth into the skillet. Bring to a boil, then reduce the heat to low and cook for 5 minutes. Turn the heat off and gently place the cod pieces in the sauce.
4. Serve over rice with Simple Chickpeas (page 122).

4 cod fillets, about 6 oz (175 g) each
2 Tbsp (30 mL) grapeseed oil
1 Tbsp (15 mL) finely chopped garlic
1 Tbsp (15 mL) cumin seeds
1 Tbsp (15 mL) ground coriander
1 tsp (5 mL) mustard seeds
½ tsp (2 mL) ground fennel
¼ tsp (1 mL) Spanish paprika
6 to 8 curry leaves
salt and pepper to taste
2 Tbsp (30 mL) tomato paste
14 oz (398 mL) can crushed tomatoes
¼ cup (60 mL) vegetable broth

MUSSELS IN COCONUT TOMATO SAUCE

MY DAUGHTER, ANOOP, loves mussels, and if it were up to her we would eat them seven days a week. She tried making this recipe herself, but because we couldn't find fresh coconut at the market she used coconut milk instead. The mussels were still fantastic. *Serves 4*

Coconut is highly nutritious—rich in fiber, vitamins, and minerals.

1. **Heat the oil** in a skillet over medium-high heat. When the oil is hot, add the mustard seeds, garam masala, Ginger Masala, fennel seeds, and curry leaves and cook for 10 seconds. Add the coconut, reduce the heat to medium, and cook for 20 seconds. Stir in the coconut milk, tomatoes, and mussels. Cover and cook for 3 to 5 minutes, or until the mussels are open.
2. Serve with Crispy Pan-Fried Eggplant with Green Pea Sauce (page 110).

2 Tbsp (30 mL) grapeseed oil
1 tsp (5 mL) mustard seeds
1 tsp (5 mL) garam masala (page 7)
1 tsp (5 mL) Ginger Masala (page 8)
1 tsp (5 mL) fennel seeds
10 to 12 curry leaves
1 cup (250 mL) grated fresh coconut (sidebar page 100) or unsweetened dried coconut flakes
1 cup (250 mL) coconut milk
1 cup (250 mL) canned crushed tomatoes
24 mussels, cleaned (remove the beard and scrub the shells)

PRAWNS WITH FRESH TOMATOES AND YOGURT

IN THE VILLAGE, yogurt was used primarily to cook one dish: curry. Early on I started experimenting and added yogurt to other dishes. My female elders would frown upon anything breaking with tradition, but once they tried my dishes they would be full of compliments. This recipe reflects my constant desire to break free from the old and embrace the new. *Serves 4*

Yogurt, provided you buy the low-fat variety, is very healthy. It contains good bacteria and is a rich source of calcium and other nutrients.

2 Tbsp (30 mL) grapeseed oil

1 Tbsp (15 mL) dried
  fenugreek leaves

1 tsp (5 mL) mustard seeds

1 tsp (5 mL) finely chopped garlic

¼ tsp (1 mL) ground cardamom

1 cup (250 mL) chopped tomatoes

12 large raw prawns, heads removed,
  shelled, and deveined

salt to taste

¼ cup (60 mL) plain yogurt

1 Tbsp (15 mL) tamarind pulp
  (page 8)

1. **Heat the oil** in a skillet over medium-high heat. When the oil is hot, add the fenugreek leaves, mustard seeds, garlic, and cardamom and cook for 20 seconds. Add the tomatoes, prawns, and salt and reduce the heat to medium. Cook until the prawns begin to turn pink, then add the yogurt and tamarind and continue to simmer until the prawns are fully cooked, about 3 minutes.

2. Serve with rice and Bitter Melon with Paneer (page 10).

PRAWNS WITH CARDAMOM AND FENNEL

ONE OF THE things my son and I love to do is to go to the wharf and get prawns fresh off the boat. One time a prawn jumped from the bucket onto my arm, and I screamed so loud it frightened the fisherman! During tests following an allergy scare, as soon as my son found out he didn't have any fish allergies, the first thing he wanted to do was go get fresh prawns so that I could make this. The licorice flavor of fennel beautifully complements the prawns. *Serves 4*

Fennel seed is high in iron, calcium, and vitamin C. It is also thought to be good for the eyes.

2 Tbsp (30 mL) grapeseed oil
1 Tbsp (15 mL) finely chopped garlic
1 tsp (5 mL) cumin seeds
1 tsp (5 mL) ground cardamom
1 tsp (5 mL) ground fennel
12 large raw prawns, heads removed, shelled, and deveined
salt and pepper to taste
¼ cup (60 mL) unsweetened dried coconut flakes
2 Tbsp (30 mL) lemon juice

1. **Heat the oil** in a skillet over medium-high heat. When the oil is hot, add the garlic and cook for about 10 seconds. Add the cumin seeds, cardamom, and fennel and cook for 5 seconds.
2. Add the prawns, salt, and pepper and cook until the prawns begin to turn pink, then add the coconut. Turn the heat down to medium and sauté until the prawns are cooked through, about 3 minutes. Add the lemon juice, then turn off the heat.
3. Serve with rice and Green Bean and Potato Curry (page 112).

160

I LOVE TROPICAL fruits such as mangoes and papayas, and I try to incorporate them in my savory recipes as much as I can. *Serves 4*

Papaya has many nutritional benefits. It is rich in antioxidants and B vitamins. It also contains the minerals potassium and magnesium and is high in fiber.

1. **Heat 2 Tbsp (30 mL) of the oil** in a skillet over medium-high heat. When the oil is hot, sear the scallops on each side. Remove them from the skillet and set aside.

2. Heat the remaining 2 Tbsp (30 mL) of oil in the skillet. When the oil is hot, add the garlic and cook for 10 seconds. Add the cumin seeds, paprika, coriander, and salt and cook for 5 seconds.

3. Stir in the tomatoes and cook until they are tender, about 3 to 5 minutes. Add the papaya and cook for 3 more minutes. Gently add the cooked scallops to the sauce.

4. Serve with rice and Pattypan Squash with Shaved Parmesan (page 106).

¼ cup (60 mL) grapeseed oil (divided)

12 medium scallops

1 Tbsp (15 mL) finely chopped garlic

1 Tbsp (15 mL) cumin seeds

½ tsp (2 mL) Spanish paprika

½ tsp (2 mL) ground coriander

salt to taste

1 cup (250 mL) halved cherry tomatoes

1 medium-sized ripe papaya, cut into bite-sized pieces

Suggested wine

2008 Sauvignon Blanc by La Frenz | After sipping this crisp, dry wine and enjoying its intense flavors of passionfruit, I knew immediately it would be a great match for this recipe, with its sweet flavors of scallops and papaya.

TAMARIND SCALLOPS

SCALLOPS ARE QUICK to prepare. The sauce is tangy (the tamarind) and creamy (the coconut), and the spices give these scallops a touch of the exotic. *Serves 4*

Tamarind (pictured opposite)is a good source of anti-oxidants, vitamin C, and minerals such as calcium and iron.

1. **Heat the oil** in a skillet over medium-high heat. When the oil is hot, add the scallops and cook them for 1 minute on each side, or until the scallops begin to turn brown. Add the ginger, garlic, cumin seeds, garam masala, and mustard seeds and cook for 20 seconds. Turn the heat down to medium.

2. Add the coconut flakes, coconut milk, and tamarind to the skillet, and cook until the scallops are opaque, about 3 to 5 minutes.

3. Serve with rice and Baked Baby Eggplant Filled with Paneer (page 10).

2 Tbsp (30 mL) grapeseed oil

12 large scallops

1 Tbsp (15 mL) finely chopped ginger

1 Tbsp (15 mL) finely chopped garlic

1 Tbsp (15 mL) cumin seeds

1 Tbsp (15 mL) garam masala (page 7)

1 tsp (5 mL) mustard seeds

1 cup (250 mL) unsweetened dried coconut flakes

1 cup (250 mL) coconut milk

2 Tbsp (30 mL) tamarind pulp (page 8)

Rice & Rotis

RICE WITH PUNJABI-STYLE MUSHROOMS

EVERY TIME I go to a farmers' market, I think I must be in heaven. So many fresh vegetables, and so many strange-looking mushrooms! Both of my kids like to pick out the oddest-looking ones, and we go home and create new recipes with them. I love the smooth texture of mushrooms—so perfect with rice. *Serves 4*

1. **Heat the oil** in a skillet over medium-high heat. When the oil is hot, add the ginger and cook for 15 seconds. Add the garam masala, mustard seeds, and curry leaves and cook for another 5 seconds. Add the shiitake, oyster, and button mushrooms, green chilies, salt, and pepper. Cook, stirring regularly, until the mushrooms are tender, about 8 to 10 minutes.
2. Serve the rice topped with the mushroom mixture.

2 Tbsp (30 mL) grapeseed oil

1 Tbsp (15 mL) finely chopped ginger

1 Tbsp (15 mL) garam masala (page 7)

1 tsp (5 mL) yellow mustard seeds

10 to 12 curry leaves

1 cup (250 mL) shiitake mushrooms, chopped

1 cup (250 mL) oyster mushrooms, chopped

1 cup (250 mL) button mushrooms, chopped

2 medium green chilies, finely chopped

salt and pepper to taste

2 cups (500 mL) cooked brown rice (see page 10)

Suggested wine

Freudian Sip by Therapy Vineyards | This seven-varietal proprietary blend has made quite an impression on me. Its citrus aromas make for a fantastic pairing with the spiced mushrooms.

BROWN RICE CAN sometimes be bland, but edamame and spices transform it. For casual meals, I often take whatever I have in the refrigerator and mix it with rice. See page 11 for instructions and tips on how to cook perfect rice. *Serves 4*

4 cups (1 L) cooked brown rice
    (see page 11)
2 Tbsp (30 mL) grapeseed oil
1 Tbsp (15 mL) finely chopped garlic
1 Tbsp (15 mL) cumin seeds
1 tsp (5 mL) ground cumin
1 tsp (5 mL) mustard seeds
6 to 8 curry leaves
½ tsp (2 mL) salt
1 cup (250 mL) frozen
    shelled edamame

1. **Prepare the rice** according to the instructions on page 11.
2. Heat the oil in a skillet over medium-high heat. When the oil is hot, add the garlic, cumin seeds, ground cumin, mustard seeds, curry leaves, and salt and cook for 20 seconds. Add the edamame and reduce the heat to medium-low. Cook until the edamame are tender, about 5 minutes.
3. Add the cooked rice to the skillet and mix well. Cook until the rice is heated through, about 2 minutes, and serve.

LENTILS AND RICE (KITCHRI)

LENTILS ARE SO healthy, easy to eat, and easy to digest, so in the village *kitchri* was made when someone in the family was sick. It was cooked with only salt, garlic, and turmeric, following the tradition of minimal spices. However, I've added coriander, cumin, and fenugreek since I love these spices so much. *Serves 4*

Lentils are rich in fiber and protein. Both the lentils and the **spices** provide impressive amounts of vitamins and minerals.

¼ cup (60 mL) grapeseed oil
1 small red onion, finely chopped
1 Tbsp (15 mL) finely grated fresh ginger
1 Tbsp (15 mL) coriander seeds, crushed
1 Tbsp (15 mL) dried fenugreek leaves
1 tsp (5 mL) cumin seeds
salt and pepper to taste
1 cup (250 mL) brown lentils
1 cup (250 mL) brown rice (uncooked)
6 cups (1.5 L) water

1. **Heat the oil** in a large saucepan over medium-high heat. When the oil is hot, add the onion and ginger and cook until the onion starts to brown, 3 to 5 minutes. Add the coriander seeds, fenugreek leaves, cumin seeds, salt, and pepper and cook for 30 seconds.
2. Add the lentils, rice, and water to the saucepan and bring to a boil. Reduce the heat to low and cover. Simmer, stirring regularly, until the lentils and rice are cooked, 30 to 40 minutes.

170

MY SON LOVES roti. I take advantage of this to get him to eat his vegetables! *Serves 4*

Basil is a good source of beta-carotene, iron, and calcium and also contains potassium, magnesium, and vitamin C.

1. **Combine all the ingredients** except the water in a bowl. Slowly add the water and mix with your hands. Add more water as needed to make a wet dough. Knead until all the dry flour is incorporated and the dough starts to form into a ball. Make sure the dough is not too hard or too soft—it should be the consistency of pizza dough.
2. Take a piece of dough about the size of a golf ball and flatten it slightly. Dust your working surface with flour so the dough doesn't stick. Using a rolling pin, roll the dough out into a thin circle (like a tortilla).
3. Place a nonstick skillet over medium heat and gently place the roti in the pan. When you see some small bubbly spots, flip the roti and cook the other side. When there are brown spots on both sides, the roti is ready. Repeat with the remaining dough.
4. Serve the roti with any of my vegetable or meat dishes.

2 cups (500 mL) whole wheat flour
1 cup (250 mL) loosely packed spinach, finely chopped
¼ cup (60 mL) finely chopped basil
1 Tbsp (15 mL) fennel seeds
1 Tbsp (15 mL) garam masala (page 7)
salt and pepper to taste
¾ cup (185 mL) water, more as needed

CHICKPEA FLOUR ROTI

THIS IS NOT your everyday, plain roti. It was made in the village only on very special occasions. It has a very nice texture but dries out quickly; freeze any uneaten rotis immediately. (They freeze well.) *Serves 4*

Chickpeas and chickpea flour are a good source of protein and fiber.

1 cup (250 mL) chickpea flour
1 cup (250 mL) all-purpose flour
2 Tbsp (30 mL) finely chopped cilantro
1 tsp (5 mL) cumin seeds
1 tsp (5 mL) ground cumin
1 tsp (5 mL) ground coriander
salt and pepper to taste
¾ cup (185 mL) water at room temperature, more as needed

1. **Combine all the ingredients** except the water in a bowl. Add the water slowly while stirring the dough, adding more as needed to make a wet dough. Knead until all the dry flour is incorporated and the dough starts to form into a ball. Make sure the dough is not too hard or not too soft—it should be the consistency of pizza dough.

2. Take a piece of dough about the size of a golf ball and flatten it slightly. Dust your working surface with flour so the dough doesn't stick. Using a rolling pin, roll the dough out into a thin circle (like a tortilla).

3. Place a nonstick skillet over medium heat and gently place the roti in the pan. When you see some small bubbly spots, flip the roti and cook the other side. When there are brown spots on both sides, the roti is ready. Repeat with the remaining dough.

4. I love serving this with a saucy dish like my Prawns with Fresh Tomatoes and Yogurt (page 158).

Desserts & Drinks

THIS DESSERT WAS served mostly after religious ceremonies and prayers, and sometimes it was made for special guests when they came to visit. My female elders would make it with whole cloves and cardamom, and I do the same thing—the spices subtly flavor the rice and aren't meant to be eaten. *Serves 4*

Cloves are a nutrient-dense spice, containing vitamin C, omega-3 fatty acids, calcium, and magnesium.

2 cups (500 mL) white basmati rice (uncooked)
4 cups (1 L) water
¼ cup (60 mL) honey
¼ cup (60 mL) raisins
¼ cup (60 mL) chopped cashews
5 whole cloves
4 to 6 whole green cardamom pods
pinch saffron
2 Tbsp (30 mL) warm milk

1. **Combine the rice**, water, honey, raisins, cashews, cloves, and cardamon pods in a large saucepan over medium-high heat and bring to a boil. Reduce the heat to very low. Cover with a lid and simmer until the rice is cooked, 15 to 18 minutes.
2. Soak the saffron in the warm milk for 10 minutes. Add the saffron milk to the cooked rice and mix it well.
3. Remove the cloves and cardamom pods. Serve warm or cold.

WE DID NOT have any electrical appliances in the village, so of course we were not able to make ice cream. The only time we had this treat was when an ice cream man would come walking through the streets, calling out loudly to sell his ice cream, which was usually made from plain milk and sugar. I tried mango ice cream for the first time when I went to Delhi for my interview with the Canadian embassy (this was right before I came to Canada). I instantly fell in love with it, with its flavors of rosewater, cinnamon, and honey. You can grind the almonds either in a food processor or with a mortar and pestle. *Serves 4*

2 cups (500 mL) whole milk
¼ cup (60 mL) ground almonds
¼ cup (60 mL) honey
⅛ tsp (0.5 mL) ground cloves
⅛ tsp (0.5 mL) ground cinnamon
2 cups (500 mL) mango flesh,
    mashed with a fork
4 drops rosewater

1. **Combine the milk**, ground almonds, honey, cloves, and cinnamon in a saucepan and bring to a boil over medium heat. Cover the pan with a lid, reduce the heat to low, and simmer for 5 minutes. Turn the heat off and allow the mixture to cool.

2. Add the mango and rosewater to the cooled mixture and combine well. Pour into an ice cream maker and process for half an hour, or pour into a freezer-safe container and freeze until the liquid is partly to fully frozen, about 3 hours. Make sure to stir every hour to ensure the ice cream stays soft and creamy.

CARROT HALVA (GAJRELLA)

THIS IS A common Indian dessert, usually eaten during very special occasions such as a wedding or the celebration of the birth of a boy. Traditionally, halva (gajrella) is full of ghee (Indian clarified butter) and rich cream. This healthy version does not have either, but it still has that same delectable flavor. *Serves 4*

Carrots are an excellent source of antioxidants and are the richest vegetable source of provitamin A carotenoids.

Combine all the ingredients in a saucepan and bring to a boil over medium heat. Reduce the heat to low and cover. Simmer, stirring regularly, until the carrots are completely cooked, about 15 to 18 minutes. Remove the cloves and refrigerate the halva for an hour. Serve chilled.

1 lb (500 g) carrots, peeled and grated
4 cups (1 L) whole milk
¼ cup (60 mL) honey
¼ cup (60 mL) raisins
2 Tbsp (30 mL) chopped pistachios
1 tsp (5 mL) ground cardamom
5 whole cloves

VERMICELLI PUDDING

ONCE, WHEN MY aunt visited from Delhi, she brought vermicelli with her. My mother prepared it as a very rich dessert with Indian clarified butter (ghee) and cream. I loved vermicelli the very first instant I tasted it. Here I've created an ultrahealthy version. *Serves 4*

Cranberries are an excellent source of vitamin C. They also contain fiber, manganese, and vitamin K.

Combine all the ingredients in a saucepan and bring to a boil over medium heat. Reduce the heat to low, cover, and simmer for 5 to 8 minutes. Serve hot or cold.

1 lb (500 g) dried rice vermicelli

4 cups (1 L) whole milk

¼ cup (60 mL) honey

¼ cup (60 mL) chopped
   toasted cashews

2 Tbsp (30 mL) dried cranberries

1 tsp (5 mL) ground cardamom

½ tsp (2 mL) ground fennel

RICOTTA PUDDING WITH CARDAMOM AND BLUEBERRY SAUCE

RAS MALAI IS the traditional equivalent of this dessert, but as with the preceding two recipes, it is traditionally made with lots of cream and butter. And I'm here to provide a healthier version that is just as delicious! *Serves 4*

1. **Preheat the oven** to 350°F (175°C).
2. Combine all the ingredients (except the garnishes) in a deep 6-inch (15 cm) square baking dish and mix well.
3. Bake for 45 minutes, or until the sides are browned. Allow to cool before cutting into small pieces.
4. To serve, place a spoonful of blueberry sauce in each dessert bowl and top with a few pieces of the ricotta pudding. Sprinkle a few blueberries on top of each serving and garnish with a mint leaf.

2 cups (500 mL) ricotta
1 cup (250 mL) rice flour
¼ cup (60 mL) brown sugar
¼ cup (60 mL) maple syrup
¼ cup (60 mL) pistachios
1 tsp (5 mL) ground cardamom (green or black)
1 tsp (5 mL) ground cinnamon
fresh blueberries, for garnish
mint leaves, for garnish

BLUEBERRY SAUCE
Makes about 1 cup (250 mL)

Place the ingredients in a saucepan and bring to a boil. Reduce the heat to low and cook until the sauce thickens, about 20 minutes. Allow to cool.

1 cup (250 mL) fresh or frozen blueberries
1 Tbsp (15 mL) brown sugar
1 tsp (5 mL) ground fennel
pinch orange zest
1 cup (250 mL) water

PARCHAD WITH RAISINS AND CLOVES

WHEN MY SON, Aaron, asks me to take him to "the castle," I know that he means the Indian temple. It is Aaron's favorite place to go because they serve *parchad* after the prayers. Parchad is made with Indian clarified butter (ghee—lots of it), flour, and sugar. Since Aaron loves parchad, I created my own version for him to enjoy. *Serves 4*

¼ cup (60 mL) almond butter

¾ cup (185 mL) flour

1½ cups (375 mL) hot water

¼ cup (60 mL) honey

¼ cup (60 mL) raisins

¼ cup (60 mL) slivered almonds

½ tsp (2 mL) ground cardamom

1. **Combine the almond butter** and flour in a saucepan and cook over medium-low heat until the flour browns, 5 to 8 minutes.
2. Whisk in the hot water and honey, mixing well to ensure there are no lumps.
3. Add the raisins, almonds, and ground cardamom and cook for 2 more minutes.
4. Serve warm or chilled.

SWEET LASSI (CHABEEL)

WHEN THE AFTERNOON temperatures would soar, several businesses would get together and create *chabeel* stands so that everyone could cool off with a free lassi. It was wonderful to see villagers uniting and making sure no one suffered from heat stroke.

Lassi was made from fresh buffalo milk, but I use yogurt. *Serves 4*

1 cup (250 mL) plain yogurt

1 cup (250 mL) 2% milk

¼ cup (60 mL) maple syrup

¼ tsp (1 mL) ground fennel

3 drops rosewater

1 cup (250 mL) crushed ice

Combine all the ingredients in a blender and process until smooth. Enjoy!

MANGO LASSI

THIS IS A cooling, soothing drink, perfect on a hot summer day or after a spicy Indian meal. My mother didn't make it very often; when she did, it was mostly because her side of the family was visiting. The ripest mangoes were set aside for this drink. *Serves 4*

The **pistachios** in this drink are a good source of copper, phosphorus, potassium, magnesium, and vitamin B6.

Combine all the ingredients in a blender and process until smooth. Enjoy!

3 medium ripe mangoes, peeled
　and pitted
1 cup (250 mL) plain yogurt
1 Tbsp (15 mL) crushed pistachios
　(I use a mortar and pestle)
4 drops rosewater
1 cup (250 mL) cold water
1 cup (250 mL) crushed ice

WHAT IS BETTER than mint and lemon as a refreshing drink on a hot day? *Serves 4*

Mint is rich in vitamins A, C, and B12. **Lemons** are an excellent source of vitamin C.

Combine all the ingredients in a blender and process until smooth, making sure the mint is evenly distributed.

1 cup (250 mL) plain yogurt
½ cup (125 mL) loosely packed
   mint leaves
1 Tbsp (15 mL) lemon juice
½ tsp (2 mL) ground fennel
salt and pepper to taste
1 cup (250 mL) crushed ice

MENUS

Weekday Dinner

Beet and Green Olive Salad | *page 22*

Mint and Ginger Chicken Kabobs
with Spicy Raita | *page 46*

Anoop's Favorite Carrots with Green Peas |
page 132

Parchad with Raisins and Cloves | *page 182*

Weekend Brunch

Spinach and Basil Roti | *page 170*

Scrambled Paneer and Asparagus | *page 137*

Green Pea Soup | *page 70*

Mango Lassi | *page 184*

Summer Patio Lunch

Fresh Summer Cucumber Salad
with Yogurt Dressing | *page 27*

Sweet and Sour Chickpeas | *page 123*

Rice with Edamame | *page 168*

Mango Ice Cream with Almonds | *page 177*

Dinner for a Special Occasion

Squash and Papaya Soup | *page 71*

Avocado and Chickpea Salad | *page 14*

Grilled Chicken with Coriander | *page 90*

Bitter Melon with Paneer | *page 147*

Chickpea Flour Roti | *page 172*

Vermicelli Pudding | *page 180*

Romantic Dinner

Coconut Curry Soup with Rice
and Lentils | *page 61*

Asparagus and Radish Salad | *page 30*

Coriander Tuna with Broccolini | *page 154*

Rice with Punjabi-Style Mushrooms |
page 166

Ricotta Pudding with Cardamom and
Blueberry Sauce | *page 181*

Teenager's Birthday Party

Kiwi and Radish Salad with Masala Chicken
| *page 32*

Zucchini and Cheese Quesadillas | *page 40*

Barbecued Indian Chicken Wings | *page 45*

Egg Curry | *page 103*

Sweet Lassi (Chabeel) | *page 183*

Dinner to Impress Your Guests

Warm Beet and Paneer Salad | *page 20*

Cauliflower and Chickpea Soup | *page 62*

Paneer Balls | *page 136*

Cod in Tomato Sauce | *page 156*

Fenugreek Chicken | *page 97*

Carrot Halva (Gajrella) | *page 178*

WHEN I DISCOVERED the amazing wineries of the Naramata Bench in the Okanagan Valley in British Columbia, I thought I had struck a gold mine. I highly recommend the wines from this region and encourage you to try them as they go so beautifully with my spices. I would like to acknowledge and thank the following wineries:

D'Angelo Estate Winery
www.dangelowinery.com

Elephant Island Orchard Wines
www.elephantislandwine.com

Hillside Estate Winery
www.hillsideestate.com

Howling Bluff Estate Wines
www.howlingbluff.ca

La Frenz Winery
www.lafrenzwinery.com

Lake Breeze Vineyards
www.lakebreeze.ca

Laughing Stock Vineyards
www.laughingstock.ca

Monster Vineyards
www.monstervineyards.com

Nichol Vineyard
www.nicholvineyard.com

Poplar Grove
www.poplargrove.ca

Red Rooster Winery
www.redroosterwinery.com

Therapy Vineyards
www.therapyvineyards.com

Township 7 Vineyards and Winery
www.township7.com

Van Westen Vineyards
www.vanwestenvineyards.com

ACKNOWLEDGMENTS

THERE ARE SO many people who have helped me put this book together, and I would like to thank them. I would like to thank Brad for supporting me and always being there to take care of the kids; Kathy Copps for helping me edit the introduction and the stories at the beginning of the recipes; Cheryl Beglaw for assisting me in putting together the spice list at the beginning of the book; Corrine Enojo for helping with the recipe editing and also with the food preparation for the photography; my lovely daughter, Anoop, and my wonderful son, Aaron, for giving me the strength to continue to pursue my dreams and for their incredible patience during the development of this book.

I was blessed to create my own family. They have wiped away my tears and given me courage and unconditional love. Much love and thanks to Marta, Candice, Indira, Paul, Rick, Bruce, Tom, Monica, Kathy, Megan, Julie, Wendy, Joye from Joye Designs, Tina, Kara, Mark, Andrea, Anita, Cheryl, and Tanya.

I would also like to thank the local businesses who had faith in me and became my partners in building my home kitchen, which enabled me to do the book photography and all of the filming of the TV segment "Cooking with Bal Arneson" (for a local TV show) there. That luxury allowed me to spend more time with my children while I worked on this book, and I cannot thank them enough. These wonderful businesses are Trail Appliances, Eurorite Cabinets, Save More Plumbing and Lighting, Rita Bellano, Andrea Fogolin, John Pisacreta Painting, Caesarstone, Solid Luxury Stone Ltd., Urban Barn, Warmly Yours, Zig Zag Tile Works, and Bellano Italian Ceramic.

Several amazing kitchen partners helped make the photography for this book successful. I would like to acknowledge Denby, Victorinox, Cuisinart, Whole Foods, and Bert Johnson Enterprises (specifically John).

I would also like to acknowledge Suki Takagi, Bill Moreland, and Ken Takagi, all from Suki's hair salon, for providing hair and makeup services for all of my media and book photography.

INDEX